RICHARD BUN
Michael Hall Rudol
before going on to st   ...university.
Since completing his PhD thesis on 'the idea
of immateriality in music', he has remained
active as a musician and writer—both of
fiction and non-fiction—his output includ-
ing numerous articles on themes as diverse as the Industrial
Revolution, angels and evolution. He lives in West York-
shire with his wife and two children.

IN SEARCH OF THINKING

Reflective Encounters in Experiencing the World

Richard Bunzl

Sophia Books

Sophia Books
Hillside House, The Square
Forest Row, East Sussex
RH18 5ES

Published by Sophia Books 2008
An imprint of Rudolf Steiner Press

A catalogue record for this book is available from the British Library

ISBN 978 1 85584 201 4

Cover photograph by Robert Blomfield; design by Andrew Morgan
Typeset by DP Photosetting, Neath, West Glamorgan
Printed and bound in Great Britain by Cromwell Press Limited,
Trowbridge, Wiltshire

This book is for all those people who have ever asked themselves whether the pictures they have in their mind's eye of the world are in any way the same as those experienced by others; and also, to what extent these same pictures are a true representation of the world as it really is.

CONTENTS

INTRODUCTION

Meditation Upon an Unknown Object

An event which remains fresh in my memory occurred many years ago when I was doing nothing more out of the ordinary than sitting alone one evening with a book resting peacefully on my lap. I had been reading something philosophical— something intended to make me think about my thinking— but had put the book down because on its own I did not expect it to be able to answer all my questions. So it was that I stopped reading in order to look up and out into the world around me.

It was night-time, the curtains were drawn, and I was sitting comfortably in a low armchair. Beside me was a table with a reading lamp standing on it. This illuminated the upturned book before spilling its light over my lap and onwards to the four corners of the room. My bed was just in front of me, a bookcase was over by the window. In the opposite corner to where I was sitting was a desk. This was covered with an array of papers, pens and pencils. Also on the desk, and displaying a sense of order which contrasted with the chaos left by me, was a spider plant. In one direction, its curved leaves caressed the surface of the desk, while in another, it sent baby replicas of itself down towards the floor.

Everything in these surroundings was clearly recognizable. No single object held any surprises for me. The room and its contents did not ask questions of me, just as I did not ask questions of them. I expected to be able to turn my attention towards any object and immediately recognize it. This was a fact I took for granted until suddenly it was no longer the case. The reason for this abrupt change was that I had noticed something directly in front of my eyes that I had not seen before. I simply did not recognize it as I did the other objects around me. Whether it was an object or an apparition, whether it was real or unreal, my thoughts could not tell me. All I knew was that my eyes clearly saw it.

When I redirected my gaze towards what I was already familiar with, my thoughts instantly connected with what I was looking at. When I turned towards the bed, I knew the bed was there right in front of me; similarly the bookcase, the desk, the chair I was sitting on and the lamp at my side. But when I returned my glance to a place scarcely more than an arm's length in front of my face, what my eyes were seeing defeated my thoughts entirely. All that my mind could muster was the idea that something unknown had appeared in front of me. Beyond that, I did not know.

The cause of this inner turmoil was a vertical shaft of light which seemed to be hovering in the space in front of my eyes. Far thinner than any thread of cotton, it was as if I saw it only by virtue of its being distinct from the darkness of its surroundings. It was more like an imaginary line in space than anything I could reach out and touch. Above it there was nothing, just as below it there was nothing. It touched neither the ceiling nor the ground. I was sure of it. And since my eyes could see no support for this apparition, my thoughts immediately bestowed upon it the quality of weightlessness. One followed the other, just as my thoughts about weight- lessness led me on to thoughts about immateriality. Nor was I able to fathom how any object could suddenly come into being in front of my eyes, apparently attached to neither floor nor ceiling. Things did not simply materialize out of nowhere. Yet whatever this thing was it could not have been there long, since it now hovered in a place where my body had walked just before I had sat down.

Even though both my eyes and my thoughts belonged to me, they did so in different ways. My eyes clearly saw it, and I knew they would not lie to me. I trusted them because they were both selfless and impartial. Not so my thoughts which could be both selfish and fickle. They were manipulative, too, capable even of taking me places I did not wish to go. They had also deceived me in the past, whether deliberately or inadvertently. They had tricked me into mistaking a falling leaf for a bird, an object's reflection for the object itself, or confusing what was just a picture with the thing it represented. I had long since come to the belief that the phrase *trompe-l'œil* (which in French means literally 'deceives the eye') was ill-conceived, since pictures which trick us with their realism do so by deceiving our thoughts and not our eyes. In reality it is our thoughts which are the true masters over our eyes, along with all our other senses. The ear still receives the sound of the ticking clock even if we do not register its presence with our thoughts; our nostrils still breathe in the scent of our surroundings even if we are not always aware of it. In such cases it is our thoughts which overlook the world at large, and not our senses. We live such examples more or less consciously every moment of our waking lives; but now my eyes saw something which my thoughts could not comprehend, however conscious I tried to become.

For a few strange moments, a part of me looked on in bewilderment as my thoughts disagreed with my eyes. Each did not believe the other. My thoughts had lost faith in my eyes, just as my eyes, without the help of my thoughts, were left abandoned. All I was sure of was that I had to look at this thing more carefully. I tried, but all I saw was a thin shaft of light which confounded my every expectation. It existed in space. I was sure of that. As I moved my head from side to side the line remained static. I, as subject, moved; while it, as object, did not. There seemed something reassuring in this. It renewed my belief that my eyes were not deceiving me and that I was not the gullible victim of some 'trick of the light'.

My thoughts raced, trawling through all that they could remember in the hope of finding something which would match what my eyes were seeing. In practice, I looked on in horror as the detritus of my memory was brought to the surface. I could not suppress what was now welling up within me, even though much of it I knew to be no more than the remnants left upon my imagination by my exposure to science fiction in its many forms. Speculation or superstition, I began to think that what was in front of me was a break in the fabric of space. The only thought which seemed to match what my eyes were seeing was the idea of a fault line in space that had somehow opened up in front of me. However unlikely that was, my thoughts were trying to tell me that light was shining through from another universe, from another dimension where it was day, just as in my world it was now night.

I wanted to test this apparition further, but wary of seeing my hand disappear into an alien world, I decided upon a safer course of action. I would direct my breath towards it and see what happened. I had come so far as to believe that I was facing something entirely immaterial. I did not expect it to move, least of all by the gentle force of my breath. Even so, I raised my chest, pursed my lips and blew. At first it did nothing, and my belief in its immateriality was confirmed. Then, as surely as I had breathed, so after a few short moments it moved, first away from me, only to return to its original position.

It moved as I might have expected an object of substance to move. I had probed it with a *cause*, and it had answered me with an *effect*. It swayed to and fro as if it were no more than a thread. I noticed that it did not stay straight, but curved as it swung. The thoughts that it was some window into another dimension rapidly retreated. I felt foolish as well as disappointed at the sudden realization that this object probably belonged to *my* world.

I looked again, and more carefully this time. It was as fine as could be, so much so that it reflected the light from the reading lamp while at the same time appearing to have no substance of its own. Human-made thread was always much coarser than this. It could not be that. I continued to probe it, believing now that it was not an object beyond the compass of my experience; rather, it was my thoughts which had been found wanting. Yet thoughts work fast. Sometimes it seems they can act more swiftly than light itself. They are able to bridge the empty space between stars, think backwards in time, forwards in time, or travel the world in an instant. To them, space and time are no obstacle. They are limitless so long as they are allowed to be free. But usually they are fettered, their wings clipped by prejudice. Not one of my thoughts had really grasped what my eyes were trying to tell them. It had all been speculation. My thoughts had indeed travelled the world and beyond, when all along the answer lay right in front of me. Then in the next instant they had grasped it. They recognized it to be nothing more strange than a thread of silk which had been spun by a spider as it descended unseen from the ceiling not far from where I was sitting. The thread emerged from the darkness of the ceiling into the cloud of light around me before disappearing again into the darkness at my feet. There was no longer any mystery.

All at once I felt something as my thoughts resolved themselves. Something within me had changed from tension to release. Not only that, but it seemed that the object, too, had been released from its spell. A door had been opened within my mind through which the spider's web had at last come in to meet me, shaken me by the hand and introduced itself. Before then, my thoughts had remained detached from the world. They had never truly met what my eyes wished to show them.

During this moment of realization, nothing had changed in terms of the impressions received through my eyes. They had remained more or less constant. Rather, it was my thoughts which had changed. A feeling that all was not as it should be had endured until such time as the impressions passing through my eyes had met my thoughts in a new feeling of resolution. Some might call this feeling of resolution as sense for truth. I could not rest until I had found it.

Such acts of recognition, I realized, must take place with every encounter that we have with the world, except most acts of recognition occur so quickly they pass unnoticed. In this instance, just because it had faltered meant that I had become more aware of it than normal. What usually took place in an instant had been stretched to such an extent that its workings had been laid bare before me. I had witnessed the act of recognition in the manner of an event in slow motion. I had been a conscious and attentive witness to the moment when an object of the world, and my thoughts about that object, had formed themselves into a unity.

The thing which had enabled me to become this *conscious and attentive witness* was that especially human quality: self-awareness. It was this which had become for me an inner light able to shine upon something which usually remained in darkness. It allowed me to look upon the sanctuary of my own being almost in the manner of a spectator. There I had seen the vulnerability of my own thoughts—that my grasp of reality hangs, quite literally, by a thread. But this was more than made up for by my experience of what it feels like to take one small yet true step towards the reality of the world.

★   ★   ★

This encounter with my thoughts and my experience of the world also taught me how philosophy can grow out of the mundane as well as the sublime. Our so-called received picture of the world is always open to question and this is reflected in the pages of this book where different aspects of human thinking and experience are examined. Though any one of the following 15 chapters is capable of standing on its own, looked at together they create a montage which I hope is greater than the sum of the individual parts. Varying in emphasis from the analytical, through the imaginative to the purely pictorial, each chapter represents, in one way or another, a real encounter with the world, while together they comprise a whole *world-view*. In addition, each of the five parts of this book is divided into three chapters in which a more substantial and analytical chapter is supported at beginning and end by a shorter and more descriptive one. These shorter chapters act both as a descriptive way-in to what follows, and a reflection upon what has preceded it. Like bookends, they help give stability to the central, larger volume standing between them.

Finally, just as rigidity can be linked to weakness, and flexibility can be linked to strength, so above all things philosophy needs to be flexible. One way of achieving this is by allowing it to live and breathe just as we do. In order for it to do that the air of our everyday experiences must flow through it. Indeed, the writing of this book has in part grown out of my belief that it is primarily through meeting our everyday experiences in a fully awake and living way that we

will begin to transform our inner life as individuals. Therefore, throughout this book I have endeavoured not to present
anything which cannot be experienced and subsequently
tested by anyone prepared actively to reflect upon their own
thinking.

Part I:
ENCOUNTERING THINKING

1. Inside—Outside

The words we see printed upon the pages of a book are outside us. The particular meaning we give to them as we read them comes from inside us.

We read while sitting inside a room which exists outside us. When we stop reading and leave the room in order to go outside, our remembrance of the room and what we have just read comes from inside us. As we move from inside to outside we always remain within ourselves.

Our sense of self exists within us. All that we reach out to with our limbs is outside us, though the intention behind them comes from within us. Through our intentions we project our sense of self out into the world.

When we walk upon soft ground, the footprints we leave behind us are impressed into the earth. Though these impressions remain outside us, they are the consequence of our intention to walk which came from within us.

Outside as well as inside, the air we breathe into us remains part of the totality of air which is outside us, while the air we breathe out again has been touched by the air which we retain inside us.

We look through our eyes out into the world. Our eyes are set within our skull; our thoughts come out to meet what our eyes offer them. What we see of the world outside us we do so by virtue of what is inside us.

Our ears are openings to the world. Some of what we hear through them is inside us; some of it is outside us. The sound we hear when we swallow comes from inside us. The sound we hear when we snap our fingers together comes from outside us.

When we open our mouth and speak, the meaning we express originates within us though the sound we produce is both outside and inside us. The words we hear spoken by others come from outside us though the meaning we bring to them comes from within us.

When we close our mouth and hum to ourself, the tones we produce sound inside us. Yet the tones and voices of our own thoughts lie still more deeply within us.

We take an apple in our hand. Inside it are seeds similar to those out of which the apple tree which bore this fruit originally grew. We take a bite from the apple. It is inside our mouth from where we experience a sense of taste. After we swallow, the apple goes more deeply into us, though by doing so it also moves outside our awareness. When it is inside us it is transformed, eventually passing out of us again.

What grows and is living outside us sustains us from inside. The skin we shed from the surface of our being was once living substance within us but has become dead substance outside us. Lifeless substance such as salt which we take into our body becomes living substance within us.

As beings of the earth we were conceived into another human being. As individuals we grew inside our mother from out of a fertilized egg into an embryo, from a fetus into a baby before being born out into the world. We took our first breath into us; we will release our last breath out of us. As mortal beings we will die back into the earth.

When we experience the sun during the daytime it is outside us. If we are to experience the sun during the night-time it is through an act of imagination which must come from within us.

The heat of the sun is something we experience outside ourselves. The warmth of our own body is something we feel is inside us.

When we are asleep, we are neither inside nor outside ourselves. In our dreams we may look upon our own body as if from the outside. When we wake up we may feel ourselves returning to our body. Though we live within a body, our thoughts project beyond it.

When we look at ourselves in a mirror, what we see from inside ourselves is our outside appearance. When we experience something which is behind our back, though we do not see it with our eyes we are able to form a picture of it from within us.

When we exchange glances with another person, we see their outside appearance from inside ourselves, just as they see our outside appearance from within themselves.

The fact of another person's existence is something we experience through impressions which come from outside us. The fact of our own existence is something we experience from within ourselves.

We experience other people as being outside us. The feelings we have for them come from within us.

Another person's notion of what inside means exists outside us. Our own notion of what outside means exists within us.

Our experiences of the world come from outside us; our sense of who we are comes from within us.

Our experience that we live within a body comes from outside our thoughts. Our experience that we are thinking beings comes from within our thoughts.

Chapter in a nutshell

- The world appears to us from two regions which are characterized as *inside* and *outside*.
- What is inside seems more connected with our thoughts;

what is outside seems more connected with our experience of the world in general. Together, each region becomes meaningful when experienced in relation to the other.

- This chapter considers how our *total experience* is in a continual state of flux.

2. The World and Our Questions

It is dusk and we stand at the head of a dark alleyway filled with moving shadows. Drizzle, illuminated by the orange flicker of street lamps, hangs heavily in the air making everything around us indistinct. Even though we cannot see them in the darkness, we call out, 'Is that you, John?' However, since we are not certain who is really there, we also call out, 'Who is there?' Because of the darkness, in reality we are not sure whether anybody is there at all, so instead we begin to call out, 'Is there anybody there?' Finally, since we receive no reply to our questions, we eventually call out 'Is there anything there?' and then wait for a response.

Each of our questions has a different focus and with it a different array of assumptions. Our first question, 'Is that you, John?', is so sharply focused that it virtually limits the scope of its answer to either yes or no. Our last question, meanwhile, is far less focused and so leaves greater scope for the answer (it also makes the curious assumption that something might be present down this dark alley which can understand our question but is not necessarily human). Each, therefore, is a compromise between clarity and lack of focus, between restricting the answer and making assumptions, between opening up possibilities and closing them down again. Whatever we ask, and however we ask it, it seems at first that our questions inevitably make assumptions, by which we mean they always take something as given without the necessary proof that it is really so.

This is certainly the case when the figure emerges from the shadows and we are able to ask them questions directly. For example, if we enquire of the figure standing in front of us,

'What do you have in your pockets?', it is very different from asking them, 'Do you have anything in your pockets?' Similarly, if we ask 'Where are your pockets?' it is quite different again from asking them 'Do you have any pockets?' The range of assumptions implicit in each question varies, though in this case they appear to diminish. The first assumes that the person has pockets and that there is something in them. The second question drops one of these assumptions, namely, that there is something in the person's pockets, but still assumes that they have pockets. The third question assumes that they have pockets even though we cannot see them. The fourth meanwhile, even though it makes fewer assumptions than the first three, still assumes many things. First among these is that there is a living person there to be asked and not just a lifeless mannequin in a shop window, or that we are staring at ourselves in a mirror. It also assumes an understanding of language, that the person asked is within earshot, that they are not deaf or can lip-read, that they are not naked, and so on and so on.

The manner in which we ask questions therefore has a bearing upon how we engage with the world. If we are not careful, our questions can take us even further away from our goal such as when we ask, 'What do you have in your pockets?' of someone who has no pockets. Though we may believe that we are taking a step towards understanding something better, the reality is that through our question we are applying yet another layer of fabrication to the world. Ideally, we might seek to focus our questions in such a way that they appear to make no assumptions at all, but this is made all the more difficult by the fact that both our questions and our answers must be expressed through words (or another form of language such as mathematics or human bodily gesture) which have their own pre-defined rules and assumptions. The very nature of our questions, and how we pose them, therefore has a profound effect upon our relationship and subsequent understanding of the world and of ourselves.

★ ★ ★

We live and function by virtue of what we can call everyday experience. As such we do not necessarily wish to step outside this so-called everyday experience in order to answer questions we did not even know existed. Generally speaking, however, we do not need to since it is we, as conscious thinking beings who pose questions of the world, and not the world which poses questions of us.[1] That is to say, it is often the assumptions implicit in our own and other people's questions to the world which make us doubt the reliability or truthfulness of our own experience.

For example, if we ask a child what warmth is, more surely than not, the question will not pose a problem for them. They will know what warmth is, even if they cannot yet express their answer in words. They will know it as a quality which they can sense. It is snugly lying in bed on a cold winter's morning; it is holding a mug of steaming hot chocolate; it is the hot summer sun on their skin as they play on the beach. Warmth is a sensation, a direct experience. We know what it is. We might also ask a child what sweetness is. As far as sweetness is concerned, so long as we have good working senses in our mouth, we all know what it is. Again it is a direct experience. It is the feeling in our mouths of sun-ripened fruit, of sugar, of honey. It is something we know and recognize even if we cannot put it into words. Indeed, words cannot really describe it anyway. A piece of fruit is sweet or sour. We know the difference and our direct experience tells us so.

However, a part of us may not be content with such answers. Another side to our nature may consider them naive, descriptive or simply vague. A part of us *feels* that feelings, descriptions and qualities are not enough. We want to know what warmth really is, what sweetness really is. What do we do? Though we are driven by just a feeling or an inclination of our thoughts, this is still enough to send us on a search for answers beyond ourselves. Through clever means we discover the changes in the substance around us which occur when warmth increases or decreases. We discover a fabric of cause and effect which coincides with our experiences of warmth. Similarly, in the case of sweetness we start to look for the chemical compounds that must be present in our mouth in order for the sensation of sweetness to arise. Yet in doing so, consciously or unconsciously, we replace the chemical changes in our mouth for the sweetness itself, or the play of molecules for warmth.[2]

The qualitative nature of our original experience seems at first inadequate in the face of explanations so thoroughly based on external observations. The trust we might otherwise place in our direct experience to explain phenomena such as warmth or sweetness is thereby undermined. And we are often willing partners in this. However, there is also another side to this. It is the view that no matter how exact and thorough we are in our observations of phenomena in general, we can never recreate in a form external to us our original experience. That is to say, the chemical changes in our mouth which are observable down a microscope are not sweetness per se, just as a chemical formula can never be sweetness either. They may tell us something of the conditions necessary for the experience of sweetness to occur, but that of course does not mean they are sweetness. A similar argument can be made for warmth in the sense that the increased oscillation of molecules is not something we can ever experience directly. Indeed, this whole argument is really one which needs no words or theories, for it is no more than a call to look more carefully at the original nature of our experience and the assumptions we make when we question how it comes about.

Both sweetness and warmth are qualities that require our participation as conscious beings. They are dependent upon our thoughts taking hold of the changes that take place in our organs of sweetness or warmth. Without the intervention of our thoughts, they are something quite different. On the other hand, the very presence of our thoughts means that we are capable of error, such as when we taste something sweet when we expect it to be sour and thus experience it as sour, or when we touch something hot when we expect it to be cold and thus experience it as cold. Because of this we are justifiably afraid that our thoughts will lead us astray, mistaking hot for cold or sweet for sour. We therefore invent means of bypassing this potential error. Yet as soon as we seek to understand phenomena in a way detached from our actual experience, something vital is irrevocably lost. In the case of warmth, it is like dropping our gloves during a winter walk. Only when our hands become cold do we realize that our gloves are missing. What we must do in order to find them again is carefully retrace our steps with a renewed attentiveness as to where we have just wandered. Or in the case of sweetness, if we lose track of our experience, it becomes something akin to gazing through the glass window of a confectioner's shop, reading the names and ingredients of the sweets inside, but never tasting them for ourselves. Really, in order to understand what sweetness is we must enter the shop and put the sweets in our mouth and taste them with as little prejudice and as much attentiveness as we can muster.

★　★　★

In an experiential sense, a good part of us knows what warmth is, what sweetness is, what light is, what darkness is. A colour-blind person knows what colour is *for them*; we know what red, green, blue and yellow are *for us*. We even know what the stars are, how the earth moves in relation to the sun, and what for us lies between and beyond them. What *we* experience on a starry night is true in itself. So long as we pose questions based upon direct experience, we know a great deal more about the world and the universe than we might normally give ourselves credit.[3] But despite this, certain questions remain. We might ask, 'To what degree is our individual experience reliable?' or 'What worth does it have?' We might also enquire: 'Is a component of individual experience shared by others?' Along the same lines we can ask, 'Is what connects us with the world around us the same as that which connects others with the world around them?' In practice, therefore, we are left questioning. We wish for demonstrable proof that our experiences correspond in some way with the objects they are seeking to comprehend. Without this assurance, we know that there can be no certainty in the world.

If, to begin with, we understand our *thoughts* to be the means by which we become aware of the existence of the world and of ourselves, this at least furnishes us with some sort of point of departure. Indeed, even if the whole world were a dream, a hallucination, a product of our imagination, we would still need to *think* our dreams, our hallucinations and our imaginings in order to become aware of them. In other words, however we imagine our relationship with the world, we must still think that relationship by means of our thoughts. This observation is one we can make of ourselves with some surety; and we do not make it lightly. Then since our thoughts have a reality *for us*, they therefore become events in an otherwise uncertain world of which *we* can be sure. How they relate to the rest of the created world is another matter and something to which we will return. That, at least to begin with, is enough.[4]

At the same time, as well as our thoughts, it also appears that we experience the world through our senses. Thus, to begin with, we appear to exist in two worlds: one which is inside us, and the other which is outside us. The outside world is brought to us through our senses; the inside world of our thoughts comes out to meet what our senses offer it. We might further characterize the world open to the senses as flowing into us like the ocean lapping upon the inlets of a coastline. Just as we cannot stop the ocean with its tides and waves, so we cannot block our senses from the world. (We can deaden the effectiveness of our senses through various means, or build defences around them. We have invented earplugs for our ears, blindfolds for our eyes, anaesthetics for our nerves, clothes to protect us from the cold. Our senses may also atrophy with age and disease, gradually crumbling away just as the defences against the sea inevitably do. Nevertheless, they continue to move and resonate with the world, though how they do so is for the moment a mystery to us.) Impressions from our body and the world beyond it flow into us in many ways and on many levels. We call these impressions *sensations*. Our ears are always open; our sense of touch is ever present and covers virtually the whole surface of our body; our eyes receive the light of our surroundings from all directions. Similarly, the sensations within our mouth, of our upper teeth pressing against our lower, of our tongue against our palate, our saliva as it flows from one part of our mouth to another: these are sensations we cannot escape. The

same may be said of the sensations produced by our breathing
as our ribs and chest are raised and lowered, the muscles
expanding and contracting, the skin on the surface of our
body moving subtly with each breath we take. However, for
all their diversity, such sensations alone do not possess the
property of discernment. Of themselves, they have no claim
to precedence over any other. What does this mean in
practice?

The world of sensations really has no more form than the
prescient chaos within the fluid of a chrysalis. For example, if
we had to live with our senses alone, we would be entirely
lost: the sun in the sky would simply be another sensation
along with the weight upon the soles of our feet; the sound of
a bird singing would be just another sensation along with the
scent in the air; the taste of food in our mouth would be just
another sensation along with the sound of distant thunder.
However, we do not live our life in this way. We are not
entirely lost. There is a spark of light within us. In the totality
of our experience, there is one thing which gives us a sense of
security and orientation. We know that the sensations of our
upper teeth pressing against our lower teeth are in some way
connected, as is our tongue as it presses against our palate.
Likewise our breathing, as the air flows into us, be it through
our mouth or our nose; we know it to be bound up with our
very existence. As we touch the world on many levels, we are
able to distinguish different objects, giving precedence to
some over·others. We know the sound of a bird from the
scent of a flower, the weight on the soles of our feet from the
sun shining in our eyes.

What distinguishes one sensation from another is not the
sense organ through which it flows, but the thought which
comes to meet it. We must wait for the forming force of our
thoughts to bring order to what our senses selflessly offer us.

They are what give us the polarities with which we order our lives. For without our thoughts we can no more hold a picture of the world than a colander can hold water. Events would pass through us as if they had never happened. We would only live life in the present, with no notion of future or past, of who we are or what we will become. Each and every impression would be washed away with the tide of every new moment of our being.

By seeking to understand our thoughts in this way, this at least gives us a point from which to further our questioning. But how best to proceed? What normally happens is that when our senses encounter something, whatever it is, our thoughts take over and bring that something into context. They do this by various means such as naming it and generally forming associations in and around it and so on. Even when we encounter an object we have never seen before, our thoughts immediately jump to help us. Indeed, our thoughts, it transpires, can often be over-zealous helpers, happily leading us along tangents through clouds of assumptions and prejudices. They are very difficult to restrain, and love to leap to conclusions or diversions wherever they can.

What happens, though, if we attempt to steer our thoughts away from their engagement with our sensations and direct them instead at themselves? The first thing we notice is that this is difficult to achieve, and that it does not happen unless we ourselves *will it to happen*. Furthermore, perhaps at first we can do it for no more than an instant. Then once that instant is passed, it is likely that our concentration will fail us and our thoughts will return to something with a more obvious sensory content. Yet during that instant, however short it is, something fundamental changes within us. When we observe our thoughts, we do not do so through our eyes, our ears or our sense of touch. In the case of thoughts, we observe them directly through other thoughts. This is also in contrast to when we, say, stroke the palm of our hand with our fingers or thumb. In a limited sense our hand is indeed sensing itself. But what makes an awareness of such sensing possible is our thoughts of the palm of our hand conjoined with those of the tips of our fingers. This is what unifies the whole experience. Without the thoughts of sensation in our fingers and our palm, no connection is made between them. Our hand does not observe itself. It is our thoughts which bridge the various sensations into a unity. Similarly, the eye cannot observe itself. When the eye looks at itself in the mirror, it does not see itself, but merely a reflected picture. An external picture of the eye is something quite different from the eye which sees. What it sees is a picture facilitated by our thoughts with the aid of a mirror. Even when we have a headache which throbs right inside our skull, we comprehend the pain as a sensation external to the core of our being, that is as something mediated to our awareness by our thoughts.

On the other hand, by using thoughts as 'sense organs' to observe other thoughts, we find that we are able to direct our attention towards an object (in this case other thoughts) without having to step outside ourselves. With no other sense organ is this possible. Expressed another way, though we do not yet know where this will take us, we notice that when we begin to consider our own thoughts using other thoughts, we do so with an activity which is of a like nature to what it is we are observing.

★ ★ ★

At first this may seem an unpromising direction for our questions since generally speaking we have a tendency to believe in subject–object relationships, that is to say in a *subjectivity* somehow *inside* us, and an *objectivity* which is in some way *outside* us. However, only relatively speaking do our thoughts take place within us since it is our thoughts which supply us with notions of inside and outside in the first place. Yet on the basis of their being inside us, we subsequently believe them to be particular to us. On the other hand, the objects and events of the world, which we place outside us, we believe to be common to all people and therefore of a general nature. However, what lies beyond our thoughts has only a claim to validity through our own individual nature, whereas our thoughts have a claim to validity through themselves. The world in its totality, we must concede, is at first dependent upon this so-called subjective nature of ours. We view it from our own particular point in space and time, coloured by the subtle variations in the acuteness or bluntness of our senses. The world, as we experience it, has a continually fluctuating nature. By the time it is mediated to us, it is already influenced by our personal feelings, tastes, opinions, the tangents our thinking takes us along, the sensitivity of our senses and the assumptions we layer upon it through the questions we ask of it. To say then, as a premise, that the world is objective, is to overstep the bounds of our own (subjective) authority. We cannot escape this conundrum by means of subject-object thinking. It is always there, continually being reinforced by the fact that the idea of an object, the very notion of a world beyond the limits of our being, is one in the first place established by our thoughts.

Just because our thoughts are capable of becoming objects for other thoughts means that they are unique in the whole compass of our experience.[5] Indeed, it is perfectly legitimate for us to begin to consider the objectivity in our own apparent subjectivity. Nor should we see this as some kind of curious tautology. Its strangeness lies simply in the fact that it is an activity we are not used to doing in our everyday lives.[6] In reality, it is something all self-aware thinking beings are capable of, even if at first it seems to be an impossibility. However, it will become a reality for us only when we make ourselves aware of a very important proviso. That is the following.

Simply directing our thoughts at other thoughts does not take us far. At worst we become like the dog which chases itself round in circles trying to bite its own tail. Whenever we attempt to think about a particular thought, the new thought displaces the old one and we get nowhere. For example, we think about our hands. When we think about our thoughts about our hands, the original thoughts are displaced by new ones. By this means we achieve a degree of self-awareness, but not any noticeable enlightenment, least of all about the nature of our hands. The objects we create as our goal (the thoughts about our hands) immediately vanish when we bring forth new thoughts (the thoughts about thoughts) with which to grasp them.

For the moment at least it seems that thoughts about thoughts are no more than a mirage we will never reach.

What we experience directly out of ourselves is that we are intimately bound to our own thoughts. This is something so obvious that we can easily overlook it. Yet confronting the obvious gives us the means of escape from the endless circle created by thinking about our thoughts.[7] We have within us a faculty that enables us to direct our thoughts, either to the manifold world of sensations or towards themselves. The wellspring of this faculty lies within us. Meanwhile, the very fact that directing one thought at another results in the preceding thought being displaced also tells us that there is a certain force behind our thoughts. This force and our faculty of being able to direct our thoughts are one and the same thing. The force which knocks one thought off its pedestal only to replace it with another is therefore something we bring out of ourselves. We can call this force the *activity of thinking* in order to distinguish it from the thoughts themselves.

This thinking activity is by definition the precursor to the awareness of thoughts: without the act of thinking, there can be no awareness of specific thoughts. Then if we are able to shine the light of our own thoughts upon the activity of thinking, we instigate a genuine transformation in our relationship both with ourselves and with the world. But this cannot be done in a haphazard way. Thinking activity is the action of placing a thought upon the pedestal of consciousness. If we think the activity of placing the thought, this itself becomes the content of the thought placed upon the pedestal of consciousness. *The activity of thinking happens. We think about it. In that instant, the actual activity of thinking, that is its genesis or mode of coming into being, becomes the content of a specifically thought thought.* There are no words to describe this process. Its veracity lies in the very fact that it cannot be put into words. But if it is acted upon, thought and thinking about thinking momentarily coincide.

In this unique moment, *a single thought illuminates its own process of becoming rather than dislodging the previously thought thought.* It becomes a self-illuminating activity in which the object in all its aspects (that is to say our own act of thinking a thought) and the thought which grasps it become one. There is no other situation in human existence where this is the case. It is a process which any clear-thinking individual can undertake.

When we turn our attention away from our thoughts in their own process of becoming and back to the impressions we receive through our senses, we immediately notice a qualitative difference. Sensations impress themselves upon us without the need for us to be active. On the other hand, with our thoughts which come to meet these sensations we must be active: the force of our own activity of thinking must run through us. This difference is something we can observe directly within ourselves, and the more we do so, the more it becomes a reality for us.

This qualitative difference arises because the so-called world at large is mediated to our thoughts from beyond our thoughts, as opposed to our activity of thinking which is mediated to our thoughts through itself. We therefore make no assumptions about the world at large other than to say that its appearance to consciousness is different from that of our own activity of thinking. In all philosophical endeavour, an awareness of this distinction is probably the most fundamental observation we can make. It enables us to become aware of how the continuous stream of sense impressions we receive from the world can only be considered to have a claim to reality; while the activity behind the thoughts which come to meet these impressions is the one dimension of our *total experience* of which we can be certain. For here, and only here, may we lay claim to an element of certainty regarding our existence in the world: that we have a consciousness of *our own activity as thinking beings*. Beyond that, and in particular how the activity of thinking relates to the rest of the world, and in what sense the *rest of the world* exists, will be the subject of the following chapters.

★   ★   ★

As an exercise, we reflect upon what happens within the sphere of our thinking when, for example, we are suddenly faced by an object such as a plant, an insect or a piece of rock about which we have no specialist foreknowledge. We can do this by approaching the object in two fundamentally different ways.

In the first instance, we reflect upon the fact that although we are able to recognize the plant as a plant, the insect as an insect and the rock as a rock, we do not otherwise possess any factual knowledge relating to it (such as its name, genus, classification and so on). In the second instance we attempt simply to open ourselves up to every possible observable aspect of the plant, insect or rock. In the case of a plant, we are able to experience the shape of its leaves and stem, its variations of colour from root through stem and leaf to flower, its unfolding and withering through space and time, as well as its relationships with everything around it. The same countless possibilities of observation are open to us in the case of an unknown insect or rock. We can achieve all of this despite the fact that we do not know what type of plant it is, what type of insect it is or what type of rock it is.

To summarize, in the first case we concentrate on what we do not know about something; in the second case we concentrate on what we are able to observe of it in an immediate way.

What we begin to achieve by this is a realization that by posing ourselves questions we cannot answer directly out of our own experience, we are in fact asking questions not of the object before us but of a body of factual knowledge pertaining to it. Finally, by turning our attention back towards the relationship our thinking has with the object in question, we also begin to reveal a tendency in the first mode of thinking to bring to awareness aspects of an object which are not intrinsic or essential to its existence. That is to say, a plant's name and genus are not essential to the life of a plant; whereas many of those aspects which are directly observable through an unprejudiced encounter with it, such as its unfolding in space and time and how it relates to its surroundings, are essential to its being.

Chapter in a nutshell

- The way we ask questions of the world appears to prejudice our answers. These prejudices arise through our thoughts as soon as they engage with the world.
- The world appears to flow into us through our senses by means of sensations. These are formless and without precedence over one another.
- Our thoughts bring form to our sensations, but also the possibility for prejudice and error.
- We begin to push back these prejudices by directing our thoughts towards our own activity of thinking.
- This chapter considers how we are able to initiate this self–illuminating activity which provides the foundation for understanding thinking's relationship with the wider world.

3. A World Without Thoughts

It is possible to separate our sensations from our thoughts only through a leap of imagination. Since we cannot become conscious of something without also thinking it, a world of pure sensory experience in which thought does not participate can never exist in our conscious minds. Thus, although we cannot ever know of such a world directly, we can nevertheless speculate as to what it might be like. If we were not beings filled with thoughts, our experiences of the world would be very different from what we are used to. They would be alien to us, strange, disjointed, but most of all, incomplete.

★ ★ ★

Our eyes would be open to the surface of this book and to everything which lies around it. Our ears would hear the sounds of traffic outside, the air as it passes our nostrils, our clothes as their fibres rub against each other. We would also be sensitive to the smells around us, to the tastes in our mouth, our tongue as it skirts our teeth and the roof of our mouth, a delicate pressure in the tips of our fingers, a coldness in our toes and the weight of our body pressing on our buttocks. We would be open to the world, though our thoughts would, for the moment, be cut off from us. We would receive but not respond, for we live in only one world: that of the senses.

We would know nothing of beginnings and endings, of borderlines or form. Light and shade, the spectrum of colours which impress themselves upon our eyes, would all flow into us with equal precedence. Though there are many objects around us, we would make nothing of them since we have no way of knowing where one object stops and another begins. The pages of this book would be a cloud of greyish white, with an array of black symbols overlaying the same space as the white, all dimpled with light and shade. At its edges, white would turn to the colour of our hands and the surface where the book rests. We would know nothing of the relationship between these colours, and what their juxta-position means. That they mark the edge of one object against another is something about which we must remain completely unaware. They are no more than splashes of colour like any other. They are simply impressions without meaning.

Nor would we have any notion of space, and since we know nothing of space, of touch or separation, near or far, up or down, we would not distinguish the sensations of our own body from those which come from beyond it. The sound of our own breathing would simply exist alongside all other sounds. Not only that, without our thoughts, we would make no distinction between the sensations coming from our different sense organs. The touch of our fingers and the smells around us would have as little relationship to us as the sen-sations we might otherwise call our feelings. These, whether they be of hunger or thirst, or indeed of joy or sadness and everything in between, would appear alongside the impressions received by our eyes from our surroundings. Our deepest emotions would be as meaningless as the fleck of grey we cannot recognize as the tip of a pencil.

We would know nothing of pencils, just as we would know nothing of ourself and what it means to be ourself. We would also be equally reticent of both our memories and expectations. Without our thoughts we would be lost. Like a droplet of water floating in the air, mirroring all that is around it, drifting with the wind, changing shape constantly, our self would be the plaything of the forces that envelop it but retaining none of the images that shine upon it. The ephemerality of all our experiences would be absolute. Our self would be empty and unable to hold onto anything. The light of the world would pass through it. It would see all but understand nothing.

As with space, so with time and any sense of continuity; without our thoughts we would live only in the present moment. Our ability to forget would be consummate. Our experience would be continuous, though we would experience no continuity. Any one experience would last no more than an instant before it was replaced by another. The blink of our eyelids might just as well last a lifetime as a fraction of a second. A cloud passing in front of the sun would not do so with movement, since without a notion of time or space we would have no comprehension of motion. A day would be indistinguishable from an hour, an hour from a second. The sun would have no relation to daytime, the stars no relation to night-time. Day and night would be no more than phases in an existence where every moment was transitory. There would be no before, just as there would be no after.

If we moved our hand to reach for a pencil, we would make no connection between our action and our wish to write something. We would know nothing of motives, just as we would know nothing of consequences. Also the weight we feel pressing down on our arm, the sound of our clothes and cracking joints as our arm moves, and the change in the balance of our body, would all be without relationship to one another. Without any thoughts to accompany our actions, we would not even recognize that it was us who moves. The movement of our own body would be as removed from us as the path of the sun through the sky.

We might open our mouth and speak; we might sing as

loud as we can. We sing so loud that our skull resonates with the sound that we produce. What we hear mingles with the drone of traffic and is lost. What we feel dissipates into a sea of sensations without borderlines. It does not help us to discover ourself. We look for the life in us, for the core of our being, and cannot find it. All is mute. When left unattended to by our thoughts, no sensation ever gains its character, its individuality, its structure. In truth, it is never really born.

Chapter in a nutshell

- By means of an imaginative study, this chapter considers how the world might appear if thinking were to play no part in our existence.
- We become aware of our surroundings when we apply our thinking to it. Without our thoughts, the world in the form of sensations would simply flow through us without structure or relationship. Most importantly, it would appear incomplete.
- By excluding it, the essential role played by thinking is thereby reinforced.

Part II:

THE GRACE OF THINKING

4. Thinking's Gift

Like a net, our thinking catches impressions from the world and brings them into relationship both with each other and with ourselves. Depending upon the *mesh of our awareness*, some aspects of the world may pass us by, just as others are caught. However, no sensation alone ever presents itself to us with any meaning or significance attached to it. If it did, the world and our relationship to it would be very different. Instead, we live between two worlds: the formless world of our sensations and the forming world of our thoughts. It is our thoughts which give our sensations their life, and we may learn from this.

Thus, everything we see has form. We recognize the characters, words and outline of this book, just as we recognize the hands which hold it, along with the skin and nails which mark their boundary. All have definition in space and are impressions imbued with meaning. Our sense of self is quite different from our experience of the objects around us. We know that the rise and fall of our breathing or the flick of our eyelids are related to us in a way that the sound of a fly buzzing against the window is not. Similarly, the touch of our fingers or the smell through our nose, each have a totally different relationship to us from the sensations we are able to call our feelings or emotions. These make themselves known to us from a source which is otherwise different from the world beyond the bounds of our body.

Though we live in the present, we are able to distinguish memories from expectations, the past from the future, yesterday from today. Our memories tell us who we are, our expectations what we wish to become. Provided we are awake to the world, a minute is different from an hour, night different from day. Our awareness of time endows us with a sense for movement. A stream of thoughts accompanies our conscious actions, just as our actions themselves are a consequence of motives of will. We sense the movement in our arm as it reaches for a pencil, just as we recognize that the motive behind this action is a wish to write something down.

Without our thoughts, all of this is absent; but with them we establish our place in relation to our surroundings, our feelings towards the rest of existence, and our will to leave our imprint upon the world. Our thoughts give us all of this. However the world presents itself to us, our thoughts are ready to bring our sensations to some sort of order. Without restraint or inhibition they make distinctions, relations, associations, contrasts, connections, separations. They do so out of habit, often with good reason; though sometimes they do so without good reason at all. That is their nature, and we must be mindful of it.

Individual experiences gain their place in the world through our thoughts and, beyond that, through our activity of thinking. Indeed, pure sensory experience comes to thinking totally naked and with a begging bowl. As such it places itself at the mercy of all the assumptions and prejudices our thoughts are capable of. The gift which is bestowed upon pure experience by our thoughts can turn to poison, leading us to false premises, false truths and false paths. Whether this gift can also bring an element of truth to our picture of the world we cannot yet say.

Chapter in a nutshell

- This chapter complements and contrasts with the previous one.

- It considers the role played by thinking in creating an ordered picture of our surroundings. It also describes how our thoughts define our sense of self, as well as other characteristics of our existence such as time and space.
- Given the power of thinking, this chapter ends by posing the question: to what extent do our thoughts create a true or false picture of the world?

5. A Forest of Christmas Trees

We are circled by trees which spread out as far as our eyes can see, and probably beyond. What strikes us first and foremost is the *diverse regularity* or *variegated uniformity* of our surroundings. This comes from the clear and simple fact that, for the most part, everywhere we look we see the same type of tree. The vast majority stand in long straight rows, with just a hint of nature's homespun chaos to break up the regularity of the lines. In one direction, we notice how all the trees appear to have been planted the same distance apart, while in another, they have grown so large and so close that we can hardly discern one from another. Nevertheless, we are still able to recognize them easily since they are of a type used commonly as Christmas trees, though where they grow densely together they also make us think of fairy tales such as Hansel and Gretel or Little Red Ridinghood. By some quirk of knowledge, we also know that they are called spruce trees, Norway spruce to be precise; while all the signs are that, strictly speaking, we are not in a forest or wood at all, but in the midst of a plantation.

The exception is a great tree trunk that lies at our feet, its jagged stump still rooted firmly to the ground beside it. We wonder what a mighty crack it must have made as its trunk was sheared in two; how the sound must have echoed into its surroundings. Otherwise, we look around to the countless upright treetops silhouetted against the skyline. In any one area, all the trees are more or less the same size, in girth as well as height. Yet for all their similarities, it is remarkable how no two trees are exactly alike. Some have broken branches, others are even without a crown, decapitated, we presume, by the wind or injured by other trees as they themselves were brought to the ground. Others have scars on their bark where deer have rubbed their antlers, a few the signs of infestation by insects. Some we even think of as more perfect than others, just because they seem to conform to our expectations for balance, symmetry and proportion—not too squat but not too lanky, a straight trunk and broad branches, not too bushy but also not too bare, and so on.

The trees around us thereby present us with remarkable similarities as well as endless variations. They are all alike as well as all being different.

We at first feel safe in our supposition that the trees really do exist beyond the boundaries of our body. We also believe that something of them flows into us through our various senses: light reflected off their surface through our eyes, the smell of pine needles through our nose, the sound made by the crunch of decaying matter beneath our feet through our ears. Sense impressions such as these in conjunction with our thoughts and all that we have learnt in our life thus far about different types of tree and how to recognize them allow us to gain information and thereby to build up a picture of our environment. And if all else fails, we know that if we so wish we are able simply to reach out and touch the trees to confirm that they are real. We can take hold of a branch, softly stroking the fronds one way, feeling the prick of the needles as we stroke it the other way. And just to make doubly sure, we can pinch our arm as we do so in order to confirm that we are not dreaming either.

At the very same time, we can also observe another apparently separate dimension to our present experience of the trees. This is made up of memories and personal associations. Where the trees are large and their lower branches are bare from lack of light, fine green needles mixed with the brown dried needles of previous years create a thick fibrous carpet which crunches satisfyingly beneath our feet. With this comes such an evocative smell that it is able effortlessly to transport us to far-away places and far-away times. If we celebrated Christmas when we were young, it might take us back to our childhood, to Christmas Eves and Christmas holidays, to decorating the Christmas tree and opening Christmas presents. If we did not, it might instead take us to fairy-tale castles or magical kingdoms set in dark spirit-inhabited forests. On the other hand, if we grew up in a city quite separate from such trees, it may take us somewhere apparently quite unconnected with where we are now. Nevertheless, we cannot deny that however hard we try to live in the present moment, our experience of the trees around us is tinged with personal memories. Even as we endeavour to absorb our surroundings as faithfully and impartially as we can, we soon realize that we cannot escape the world of our own thoughts and the flood of associations and memories which come with them.

So it is that we find within our own experience a number of interpenetrating *worlds*. There is the world of our own personal thoughts and memories in relation to these trees, which are unique to us and which only we can have. There is also the world of the trees themselves as they surround us in their physical reality. But somewhere between these two extremes is the way in which we are able to recognize the trees as all being of the same type despite their differences, as well as the way we are able to recognize each tree as being different despite their being of the same type. This seems at first to be an experience which is revealed to us from within ourselves but which is also intrinsic to the trees themselves. As such, it is something like a third world which is *within and beyond* both the trees and ourselves.

★ ★ ★

Based on all that we can see and touch, we consider ourselves entirely justified in the belief that the trees exist and that information regarding them flows into us through our various sense organs. But how does this belief stand up to scrutiny?[1] Our senses are constantly open to a plurality of impressions. Countless shades of green and brown engulf us. Our senses alone do not discern single needles, branches or trees. They know nothing of such distinctions. To them the world is formless. Instead, they see everything and in so doing are unable to recognize the objects and the relationships we might otherwise take for granted.

We turn our attention in one direction and recognize a large mature tree. We turn our attention in another direction and recognize a tiny sapling. The actual sensory impressions we receive from each direction are very different, and yet we are able to overcome those differences and in each case recognize that we are beholding not only a tree but trees of the same type. Furthermore, when we look in one direction and see a tree, then look in a different direction and see another tree identical to the first, though the sensory impressions we receive from each direction are very similar, we are still able to overcome those similarities and in each case recognize that we are beholding different trees.

What strikes us then is that, amidst both the diversity and regularity of our surroundings, we are nevertheless able to make the most subtle of distinctions between our manifold sense impressions. In each and every case, what enables this to happen is the fact that our thoughts come out to meet our sensations. The trees in all their multiplicity confront us as sensations; the thoughts which bring these sensations to order emerge from somewhere which at first seems disconnected from the world to which our senses are open. We might believe that our thoughts are something different, that they are of a dissimilar nature to the plantation itself. Indeed, it seems at first that the trees are one thing; our thoughts about them are something else. However, this immediately begins to change when we remind ourselves that all our notions of inside and outside are themselves thoughts. Any notion that our thinking takes place within us or that the world is outside us will therefore also be a product of our own thoughts. Furthermore, the same can be said for anything regarding the specific functionality of our senses. Without our thoughts we cannot differentiate between the sight of green and brown in front of us or the pressure on the soles of our feet.

If we continue our wanderings with this in mind, we become open to the possibility that the trees and the life of the plantation may not be so removed from our thoughts after all. As we wend our way between the trees, absorbing them as best we can, we might, on occasions, feel that notions of separation, of inner and outer, are not entirely appropriate to our thoughts and how they make themselves present to us, or indeed to the trees themselves. Another dimension to the trees which is different from that received through our senses may well make itself known directly through our own thinking. However, what we can observe unequivocally is that something emerges into our consciousness that is directly related to the trees; and it is something that can never be accounted for through sensory experience alone.

What is the nature of this dimension of our thinking that comes to us unaided? The possibility to differentiate and then recognize our surroundings comes from somewhere other than the sensory experience of those same surroundings. Rather, it is the thought *tree* that enables us to recognize the different trees around us as such. The sensory experience of the tree in all its diversity calls forth thinking activity; and the warp and weft of this activity is of an *ideal* or *conceptual* nature. In this case, the *idea* or *concept* of a tree emerges into our consciousness as a formative force in its own right.[2] It enables us to recognize the otherwise disparate sensory impressions as a tree. It unifies them through giving them relationship to one another, as well as limiting where they start and where they stop.

★   ★   ★

This plantation surrounds us with many things. We can direct our gaze so as to gain a general impression of our environment, or we can focus our attention upon details. (We can also daydream about events taking place many miles away or reminisce about happenings long since passed, and thereby scarcely take in anything of what is around us.) If we try to take in the whole scene, we may not distinguish details such as single pine needles, even though the overall impression of green we receive is made up of them. Similarly, we might look upon this same plantation from a great distance (say from an aeroplane), and still be able to recognize it as a forested area, as opposed to the surrounding fields and urban areas, even though we cannot make out individual trees. However, when we are standing right in their midst, our focus of attention can go in various directions, either towards generalities or towards details. We may choose to take in the shape of individual pine needles, the texture of a tree's bark, the shape of its trunk or branches, the pointedness of its crown, the breadth of its lower branches; or we can shut our eyes and concentrate upon the tree's smell or listen to the creak of its branches. In fact, as our body remains motionless we are able to consider all manner of things simply by changing the focus of our attention.

As we do so, our eyes may twitch while their lenses move to focus on what they are aimed at; but this is not the case with our ears or sense of smell, which are virtually always open to the world. For whatever the reorientation of our senses, the most fundamental changes takes place in our consciousness. Our thoughts are somehow able to direct themselves in order first to select and then to highlight specific sense impressions from the multiplicity of experiences to which they are open. We have the faculty for combining clusters of sense impressions from out of an otherwise chaotic sense-scape into specifically recognizable objects. We bring these objects into form; indeed, we might go so far as to say that we bring them into being.

The process of directing or focusing our thoughts in a particular way may be summarized by the noun *intentionality* or the verb to *intend*.

★   ★   ★

Our thoughts also play an integral role in helping us to recognize as similar what to our senses is otherwise quite dissimilar. For example, the thought *tree* may also be seen as encompassing all parts and all characteristics of every tree: from the child's rough crayon drawing to the tree at the end of the garden; from the photograph of a tropical tree we have never seen before to a cheese plant or weeping fig grown as house plants; from the mythical tree of life or the trees in the Garden of Eden to purely notional trees such as a family tree.

What this means in practice is that, although the sense impressions we receive from the pages of an *Illustrated Guide to Trees* we happen to have with us bear no resemblance to the sense impressions we receive from the living tree in front of us, we are still able to recognize the same tree from the pages of this book despite the fact that the picture there bears little resemblance to the tree *in real life.* Also pictured in this book are other types of tree: oaks and weeping willows, copper-coloured beeches, monkey-puzzles and sinewy yew trees. Then just to add to the diversity, some of the trees are illustrated by photographs, others by coloured paintings, a few by black-and-white drawings: static two-dimensional representations of things which are never still and which grow in the dimensions of space, sometimes to enormous sizes. And yet these miniature pictures are of help to us. They enable us to recognize trees we have never even seen before.

A part of us recognizes in each of them something which belongs generically to the same class of object, in this case trees. Specifically, we may call the idea that encompasses all aspects of 'treeness' in every conceivable context the *universal concept*, tree. This *concept* of a universal concept covers every type of tree imaginable. In any situation, as we shall see, it is able to adapt itself so as to bring form to the sensory impressions then confronting our thoughts. We can begin by describing this as a qualitative judgement, since qualitative criteria are what enable us to recognize every conceivable tree as being conceptually related. On the other hand, to our senses and therefore our raw experience, as we have seen, all trees are outwardly different from one another (even those which appear identical, since these must exist in a different space and be made of different substance from the other). In summary, therefore, we might provisionally define the act of recognition as *the interrelating, by qualitative means, of things which are experientially or sense-perceptibly distinct.*

★   ★   ★

During our everyday encounters with the world we do not experience this universal concept directly, but specific forms of it. In practice, what this means is that, say, botanically speaking, the concept *tree* is something more specific than *any* and *every* tree. It does not include a family tree, a child's drawing or an artificial Christmas tree made from tinsel. Similarly, we can be more particular in differing ways. Our concept of tree might include only those trees actually living and growing. A further concept of tree might limit us only to those trees that are evergreen; then to those with an upright conical shape; then to those with stiff pointed needles which grow from the sides of each twig. Further characteristics might eventually lead us to the idea of those trees which have been grouped together under the name spruces. Even then there are still more than 50 of these. It is only with some final refinements of our concept, *tree*, that we come to recognize the tree in front of us as a Norway spruce.

Having done so, having honed the universal concept, *tree*, to something quite specific, we then notice that since no two Norway spruce trees are exactly alike, this concept, too, moulds itself to cover all of these. In doing so, the universal concept *tree* contracts so as to bring to form the specific Norway spruce in front of us; but when we turn to one of the saplings nearby, the concept Norway spruce transforms so as to enable the recognition of Norway spruce trees in their many diverse forms. In this way, the universal concept *tree* shows itself to be infinitely malleable. It is also through such observations as these that we begin to experience how the conceptual world, of which the universal concept *tree* is a member, through acts of recognition is united with the world of sensations. For it is through acts of recognition that one concept transforms into another, contracting and expanding and thereby bringing to order what our senses offer to thinking.

The process in which a universal concept such as tree is honed down until it can bring together the sensory content of a specific tree may be summarized by the noun *indivi-duation*, or the verb to *individualize*. A universal concept must be individualized in such a way that it conforms with the sensations towards which the concept is intended. If it is not individualized, those sensations must remain formless and therefore will not come to our awareness. Indeed, if we lack the means of directing our thoughts, our experiences will remain adrift in a sea of formlessness; then if we lack the means to access a universal concept which can be indivi-dualized so as to match our experiences, they will also lack clarity and focus. In this sense, the two processes of inten-tionality and individuation (or intending and individualizing) are essential to our forming of recognizable pictures of the world. *They are the in-breathing and out-breathing of our life of consciousness.*

We live this in-breathing and out-breathing of our con-sciousness in many ways and through many examples. We do not intend our thoughts towards every object, and nor do we individualize every concept available to us. If we did, we would experience a proverbial everything and nothing. For example, even though we cannot block out the smell of our surroundings, we are not always conscious of it. What this means is that if our current thoughts are directed elsewhere in that moment we do not bring forth any concepts relating to smell. For this to change requires a shift of focus or an intending of our thoughts along with the individualizing of a concept specific to the notion of smell. Similarly, we cannot block out the sounds of the forest since our ears are always open to them. But we are certainly not always conscious of there being sounds. Nor indeed do we see everything in front of us that there is to be seen. We in effect pick and choose, though some of the time a sense impression forces itself into our awareness. We might not hear the sound of beetles scurrying across the forest floor, but we will certainly hear a shotgun going off if it is near enough since it will force itself upon our awareness. However, if the shooting goes on for a sufficiently long time, even if it remains very loud, after a while we may begin not to hear it either. Similarly with smell, it may have struck us upon our arrival but after a little while we may not notice it at all.

With every step that we take, the focus of our attention seems to change. We have heard that there are deer in this forest. We might wish for the thrill of seeing them in the wild, so our eyes are all the keener in the hope of spotting one. We know what we are looking for since we have already been told that it is red deer which roam here. We know from pictures and visits to country parks what they look like, especially their reddy-brown coat and branchlike antlers. We also know they could be anywhere, that we might stumble upon a herd of them at any time.

We have a picture of these deer which we hold in our mind. We believe that it will help us when the time comes to glimpse one of these shy and secretive animals, to distinguish it from out of the dense tapestry of trees that surrounds us. Then suddenly, in a small clearing a short distance away, we think that we see one. We recognize the curve of its back, its raised head. We are not quite sure whether we can see its antlers or not. Perhaps the angle is not right for us to see them, or the animal ahead of us is a female. Even so, we continue to step towards it, maintaining the picture of the deer in our mind's eye. As we come closer and closer, we expect it to move, to raise its head towards us, to look at us for a moment before darting away into some less trodden part of the forest.

We get closer and closer. With each step that we take towards it, we expect it to disappear into the undergrowth. When still it does not move, we begin to have doubts about what it really is. We hold on to the idea that it is a deer for as long as we can. We do so until we can hold on to the idea no longer. In that moment the concept *deer* rapidly retreats from our thoughts, leaving what our eyes see in front of us in a momentarily formless state. We realize that this thing in front of us really looks nothing like a deer at all. Only when we individualize the concept *tree* in the manner specific to what our eyes are seeing, and not as a deer, do we see it as a fallen tree trunk. Though its bark is a reddish brown, half rotted away and propped up above the ground in such a way as to look a little like the spine of an animal, we soon realize how we have been fooled.

Though we remain aware of the danger of this type of auto-suggestion, we cannot help ourselves from noticing things which might after all be deer. Indeed, it still strikes us as remarkable how many fallen trees and branches look just like deer. But, we remind ourselves, as well as deer we have also been told that there are woodpeckers. We do not necessarily expect to see them, but are hopeful that we will at least hear their fast repeating pecking sounds. Our attention is thus temporarily directed towards the hearing of one sound, and one sound only. We do not expect to hear the song of the woodpecker since we know it is not very distinctive. But in not expecting to hear that, we do not hear any of the other birdsong either. The calls of various birds fill the air, of finches, blue tits, great tits, and many others. But our thoughts are simply not receptive to them. We have primed our thinking to hear only a mechanical sound, and in doing so hear only the regular patter of our footsteps, the distant buzz of a chainsaw, the rumble of heavy logging trucks. Only later, when someone asks us about the birds we heard, do we realize that our attentiveness for one thing must have clouded our receptivity to the calls of all the other birds.

Also in the back of our mind is the thought that perhaps this forest is inhabited by spirits, that some supernatural forms of life live alongside the life we can see and touch. For this we have no preconceived notion other than what we recall from children's story books, of Victorian winged fairies sitting on water lilies, drawn in pen and watercolour, or alternatively the imagination of film-makers rigidly captured in celluloid. None of these do we really believe, and therefore do not expect to find. As a consequence, even if such things exist, we do not think them into being; and through not thinking them, we can never become aware of their presence. Just as we are unaware of the many bird calls because our thoughts are directed elsewhere in a form of tunnel vision, we muse upon the fact that a whole dimension of existence might pass us by because we do not know how to think it into our consciousness.

★   ★   ★

We look upon one tree, then another. In each case, the universal concept tree is individualized. This universal concept is something which can never arise out of our sensations. As such, it stands in stark contrast to our present sense-filled encounter with a tree, whether this is imagined, remembered or experienced in the present moment. This present form of the concept *tree* has all the characteristics of something that is personal to us. It is entirely different from what we have called here the universal concept in that it is mingled with all manner of associations that are unique to us. If we are a trained botanist, we will consider trees differently from if we are a child. If our eyes are weak, our individualized concept may be blurred at the edges or out of focus; if we are in some way colour-blind, it may lack certain contrasts of colour. If we have no sense of smell, it will be lacking in this dimension; if we are completely blind, it will inevitably be influenced by this. All these differences are either acquired through our individual circumstances in life or they are conditioned by our physical constitution. Yet for all these differences the primal force behind our faculty of recognition, behind our ability to recognize a tree in the first place, is beyond our individual circumstances in life and is not conditioned by our physical constitution. It is something which is universal.

It is not for us to remember the first ever time we recognized a tree. What we can do, however, is work backwards from our own present experiences of trees in their manifold forms. What we thereby begin to realize is that our individual experience is really a condensing into a specific form of something which is beyond ordinary sense experience. *This something is our activity of thinking.* Like the setting sun facing the rising full moon on opposite sides of the horizon, where one is illuminated by the other, so our sensory experience is illuminated by our thinking. It is as if we stand between sun and moon. Our sense experience is like the moon: without the light of the sun we will not see its outline, its form, its details, its wholeness. Meanwhile, our thinking is like the light of the sun. Without something upon which to shine, we will not see the light which emanates from it. The light needs substance in order to make itself visible to us, in order to give it form, just as substance needs light to shine upon it in order to make it visible. Therefore, just as we stand between sun and moon, we stand between our thinking as activity and our sense experience. Then where shining light and reflected light mingle, we recognize our specific thoughts and ourselves as individuals.

These are the two mysteries of our existence. A light like the sun shines from somewhere which is both within us and also beyond us; for although this light appears to shine from within us, it does so on the basis that we are a part of the world in its totality. However, this forming principle, that we have called here a universal concept, is not observable through ordinary sense experience. Rather, it arises immediately prior to the forming of our personal sense-filled picture of something. As such, it is observable only in such moments of self-reflection when our thoughts are intended towards the forming of our thoughts, that is to say, towards the activity of our own thinking. Furthermore, in its infinite malleability, the universal concept *tree* also touches all other concepts, thereby creating a link to a type of *total existence in a universalized form.*[3] Then, from out of this total existence in a universalized form, the universal concept *tree* is individualized. It loses its universal attributes and becomes fused to the specific sensory experience of the tree standing just a short distance away from us. The ideal tree is lost to the specific tree of our sensory experience.

Eventually we return to where we began, to the place where the trunk of a fallen tree lies at our feet, while beside it its roots and a jagged tree stump remain firmly planted to the ground. Here we begin to realize that our thoughts are so intimately connected with the world at large that their presence or absence plays directly upon how an event unfolds. In particular, we imagine what a sound this tree must have made as the wind, we presume, brought it crashing to the ground. But we were not there to hear it; indeed, probably no one was. What, though, would have happened if we had been there to hear it? We ask ourselves this question: would it have taken place just the same?

At first the question seems absurd. Then we begin to

reflect upon it in conceptual terms. The event has no consciousness of itself. It has a beginning and an ending in so far as one moment the tree is standing while the next it is lying on the ground. In this sense it has a beginning and an ending. It must therefore also have a duration. Spanning this duration is the sound the trunk must have made as it snapped and came crashing to the ground. While the event has a beginning and an ending spanning a particular duration, linked to which is the sound which must have echoed into the surrounding forest, in the absence of a thinking being, each moment of the event passes on to the next without relation to what has gone before. The beginning is already passed when the ending happens. Conceptually speaking, the individual components of the event are not linked. The event still takes place, but without any conceptual unity. The beginning is not unified with the ending. However, when we are there as a conscious witness, we think the various parts of the event into a unity. The beginning is held in our consciousness through until the ending. Our consciousness spans the event and conceptualizes the stream of impressions into a unity. In this way, something is brought which, in our absence, simply would not exist. But this thing which is brought is not arbitrary. For although its origin is in a universalized form which is then individualized by us, it nevertheless seems to grow out of the event itself. It is as if our thoughts add something, that conceptually speaking the happenings of the world are not complete without us. Indeed, what thinking brings is a *companion event* to the event itself, which in our absence would not otherwise be there.

Such a notion as this suggests a deep connection between the unifying concepts which are the basis of thinking and the world as we experience it through our senses. What is more, this companion event is by no means detached from the world. On the contrary, it brings something so integral to the world that it is possible to suggest that any occurrence is not entirely complete without some thinking presence being there to participate in it. In these terms, through our thinking we contribute to the unity of the world. But this is only the case when we consider our thinking in a particular way: as an activity that touches a conceptual world in a universalized form, out of which our specific and individualized thoughts are drawn. Then, through the activity of individualizing this conceptual world, through making it something specific to us, we become a bridge between two worlds: the sense world and a conceptual world.

★   ★   ★

As an exercise, we allow ourselves to daydream, in so far as daydreaming is a state in which we think about things that are not immediately connected with our current surroundings. When we are indoors we dream about being outdoors; when we are outdoors we daydream about all the things we could do when we are back indoors. Similarly, when we are at work we might daydream about the things we can do when we have finished work, just as when we are not at work we might allow our thoughts to be taken over by all that we need to do at work.

From this state in which we are awake in ourselves but asleep to our surroundings, we consciously endeavour to observe ourselves waking up to what is currently around us. That is to say, we try to make as conscious as possible the transition from being largely oblivious to our surroundings to the condition of being fully awake to them. In practice, however, we will come to realize that we do not become aware of the totality of what is around us, but only parts of this totality. Specifically, we do this by directing our thoughts through our senses. That is to say, above all things we should notice that we have to think the object in front of us in order to become aware of it;

that we have to think the sky above our head, the ground beneath our feet in order to make their existence conscious. If we do not direct our thoughts, we remain asleep to our surroundings even though our senses remain open and impressionable to them.

Just as we are able to realize that awareness of something is dependent upon the directing of our thoughts towards it, so as we revert back to a state of daydreaming we can feel the retreat of our thoughts from our senses. We thereby return to a condition which is less an engagement with our immediate surroundings and more an internalized form of experience. Meanwhile, by becoming aware of the transition between these two states, we will come to realize how, in our everyday lives, we not only fluctuate between different levels of wakefulness but also what it means to be truly awake as well as to be asleep to the world around us.

Chapter in a nutshell

- We are able to recognize the differences between similar objects such as different types of tree.
- We are also able to recognize the similarities between objects that are otherwise different, such as trees of the same type or trees in general.
- In addition, when faced with a tree, we can change the focus of our attention, such as between its trunk, branches or individual leaves. *Intentionality* is the act of directing consciousness in this way.
- This chapter considers how the act of recognition involves *individualizing* a *universal concept* into a specific inner picture of the object concerned.

6. Touching the Night Sky

Our earthly surroundings are so dark that our own body is little more than a silhouette with outline but no detail or colour. The sun is directly beneath our feet, and the moon somewhere along with it. The place where we stand is high upon the surface of the earth, away from the transitory lights and fires of human endeavour and industry. There is darkness from our feet to the arc of the horizon; but we do not feel ourselves to be alone. For when we look up into the space above our head, innumerable points of light make their presence known to us. In our mind, we call these points of light stars. That is the word we have been taught to use. The sound of this word, *stars*, gives them a name, even if it does not really describe them, since they are not sound or word in an audible sense, but something entirely different. We also know that in French they are called *étoiles*, in German *Sterne*; in Latin *stella*; and though we are sure that every other language in the world must have at least one word to ascribe to them, we cannot know them all.

We do not recall the very first time we became aware of the stars. Perhaps we once asked our parents, 'What are they?', as we pointed our hand skywards. No doubt they would have told us that we were pointing at what are called stars. But we would not have known to ask if we did not already have some inkling of their presence. Even today, we still know that they are there whether we give them a name or not, but only so long as we make ourselves conscious of them. Our eyes may receive their light, but if our thoughts do not take hold of it our inattentiveness becomes like a cloud which blots them from view. But when we do take hold of the impressions we receive from a single star and begin to think of it in relation to those from other stars, the world and our relationship to it suddenly undergoes a change.

We see a point of light from one direction; we see another from a different direction. We also experience the darkness between them. The darkness is as tangible to us as the light of the stars. In the absence of darkness, we do not experience their light (as we know from the daytime when we see no stars); in the absence of starlight, we would not experience the expansiveness of the darkness. Together we experience the separation between the light and thereby give the darkness a form. Through bringing the stars into relationship with one another, we bring a tapestry of qualities to the sky which would not otherwise be there. When we look this way and that we experience relationships and therefore qualities. These groupings of stars and their relationships have a name. They are called constellations. And each constellation has its own quality.

Without us the stars would undoubtedly still shine. They do not rely upon us for their existence. We can also take a photograph of the night sky and see the stars reproduced there. But this is not the case with the constellations. These are of a very different nature since they are dependent upon our own thinking in order to come into being. The photograph more or less reproduces what our senses see; and like our senses, the photograph is without consciousness of itself. Without consciousness, it has no sense of relation. Without relation, each point of light can never become part of a constellation. As with the sky above us, so too with a photograph of the sky, without our thinking presence, a dimension of form is lost. The photograph does not itself reproduce relationships; and the constellations, in their essence, are nothing but relationships. Yet if we bring our thinking to the connections between stars, whether in the sky or upon the printed page, something tangible is added which in our absence would not be there. When we bring into unity what is otherwise quite separate, the world in its totality changes.

The difference between the stars and the constellations is that one we see with our eyes, whereas the other we think with our thoughts. The stars have only a claim to reality through the sense impressions we receive through our eyes. Of their nature and relationships *out there* we can only speculate. The constellations, by contrast, are objects with which we are intimately connected. They are not a claim to reality, but reality themselves in that they arise through our own thinking activity – that aspect of our being upon which our whole reality rests.

We look up and see the Plough only to follow an invisible path across the northern sky, past the North Star, until our attention reaches the crown of Cassiopeia; if we are in the southern hemisphere we look up and see the Southern Cross only to follow a short but invisible path to the underbelly of the Centaur. For our thoughts, distance and separation are no obstacle; and since we do not see these constellations in the same way that we see the stars, we cannot really consider them as something external to us, even though a part of us projects them out into space, far, far away. We see the Plough; we see Cassiopeia; but only when our thoughts are active. Yet this activity is an occurrence of the world. It is made up of a stream of events of a conceptual nature, of concepts being individualized by us into the living pictures of our present consciousness. The sky would not be the same without it.

What we see of the stars which make up these constellations changes continually. With our naked eyes they flicker in the atmosphere which encircles the earth. Clouds and the vapour trails of aeroplanes darken the sky in front of them, perhaps making them disappear entirely. Through one type of telescope all manner of wonders might be uncovered. Through another we might gain yet more information that changes the way we picture them for ourselves. All the while, the great hemisphere of the sky rotates, so that the angle of our gaze is constantly shifting. The Plough and Cassiopeia can appear high or low in the sky, inverting themselves as they do so. Indeed, if the stars of the night sky did not move, the world and our relationship to it would be a very different place. Yet for all these changes, the shapes defined by the stars in the sky are never foreshortened or lengthened, but remain constant. Their constancy in the midst of their continual movement is part of their nature, whereas in the spheres of the moon and planets there is continual change.

Through their constancy, the constellations also attain the quality of universality. We experience this each time we intend our thoughts towards them and their inner nature is first revealed and then made personal to us as a deed in the world. As phenomena, we experience them as they truly are. That another person may group stars together in entirely different constellations is an act of their own cognitive freedom. Nevertheless, all such groupings are real in so far as they declare themselves directly through our thoughts. They are not something remote and open to speculation. On the contrary, they have a claim to an absolute immediacy so long as we reflect upon their manner of appearance within the realm of our thoughts. Then, with the sun beneath our feet, we see the world more clearly as it makes itself known from within us instead of from outside of us. Unlike the stars and the objects of the world of which we just see the surface, with the constellations we suddenly experience their inmost nature. Out of all the phenomena of the world, rather than being the most remote from human existence, for thinking they become perhaps the closest things of all.

Chapter in a nutshell

- We look towards the stars.
- By thinking the darkness between them, we bring the stars into relationship with one another. The resulting forms we call constellations.
- We suppose that the stars would still shine without us; the constellations, meanwhile, seem to exist by virtue of us thinking them into being.
- Similarly, the stars appear to exist beyond the bounds of ourselves, while the constellations appear to exist more within us.
- This chapter considers the different claims to reality of these two forms of object.

Part III:
THINKING THE INVISIBLE

7. Light and Darkness

A single unlit candle chimes with the darkness of the room in which it stands. When out of the darkness a match is struck and touches the dry wick, melting the wax and taking hold of the flame, a light is first born and then sustained. It is as if this ever-changing point of activity bursts forth, expanding towards the corners of the room.

When we move our hand towards it, we feel the light as heat on our skin. It arouses our sense of touch, just as it enlivens our sense of sight. One sense seems to confirm the other. We touch and see together, and therefore know that the candle flame is real.

The light has its centre in the rising flame, between the transparent blue cup at its base and the orange-yellow bud of transforming substance which fills it. From there it radiates out towards the walls, the floor and the ceiling. But our hand also casts a shadow upon the walls. As we move it around the candle flame, the shadow moves seamlessly with it just as new light reaches where the shadow once stood. On our palm which faces the flame, the lines and crevices of our skin show many shades of light and dark. But the light also passes between our fingers, only to tease us as it outlines different shapes upon the wall. It cuts the darkness, expanding inexorably as it does so.

However, this act of transformation from light to dark also bestows a gift. This gift is colour. Wherever the light meets the substance of the world there is colour. Where the light meets itself in the activity of the candle flame there is colour too. The light that spreads from the flame then takes its offering with it, giving countless subtleties of hue to the objects it meets. We see the light as it catches the hovering dust; we see it as it finds the many objects of the room; we see it as it comes upon the walls, the floor and the ceiling. We see it the instant it relinquishes itself to colour; we see it, though in itself it seems that we do not see it at all. However hard we look, we do not see the light in its state of betweenness, as it is of itself. We are witness only to its moments of meeting; where it passes untouched, the light is not only colourless but is less than colourless. It is invisible and therefore a mystery to us.

★   ★   ★

A single unlit candle chimes with the darkness of the room in which it stands. When out of the darkness a match is struck and touches the dry wick, melting the wax and taking hold of the flame, the darkness begins to retreat and die. It is as if the sudden absence of darkness releases this ever-changing point of activity, drawing it out towards the corners of the room.

When we move our hand towards it, we feel the receding darkness as heat on our skin. It arouses our sense of touch, just as it enlivens our sense of imagination. One sense seems to confirm the other. We touch and imagine together, and therefore know that the darkness is real.

The darkness remains most intense at the outer reaches of the room, in its recesses and corners which are free of light. From there it dissipates inwards to where the lighted candle stands. But our hand also protects the darkness upon the walls. As we move our hand, new darkness is seamlessly created just as the old darkness is overrun by light. On the back of our hand which faces the darkness, the rounds of our knuckles and the folds of our skin remain in shade. But the darkness also passes beyond our fingers in the direction of the flame. There it is further diluted by light until it seems not to be there at all.

However, this act of transformation from dark to light also bestows a gift. This gift is colour. Wherever the darkness meets the illuminated substance of the world there is colour. Where the darkness meets itself in the darkest recesses of the room there is not. But the darkness which ventures towards the light does so with an offering: to transform the light and thereby give countless subtleties of hue to the objects it meets.

We see the darkness as it catches the hovering dust; we see it as it touches the many objects of the room; we see it as it dissolves away along the walls, the floor and the ceiling. We see it the instant it relinquishes itself to colour; we see it, though in itself it seems that we do not see it at all. However hard we look, we do not see the darkness in its state of beyondness, as it is of itself. We are witness only to its moments of meeting; where it passes untouched, the darkness is not only colourless, but is less than colourless. It is invisible and therefore a mystery to us.

★ ★ ★

Where the light meets the darkness, and the darkness meets the light, the mystery of both is revealed to us. Before this meeting, the light's quality of invisibility has something of the nature of darkness, while the darkness' quality of invisibility has something of the nature of light. Indeed, in the case of light it is not the light that we see, but the darkness as it penetrates the light; while it is not the darkness that we see, but the light as it penetrates the darkness. It is the darkness which releases the light, thereby making the light possible, just as it is the light which releases the darkness, thereby making the darkness possible. Without the darkness there would be no light. Without the light there would be no darkness.

Light is like darkness until it touches substance, however fine that substance is. Meanwhile, substance is like darkness which once was light. Yet only at the instant of meeting does light reveal the side to its nature which is familiar to us.

Light, we observe, cannot escape becoming ever more like darkness. Yet darkness is the stuff out of which the light is born. Which came first, the light or the dark? Was the light born out of the darkness or the darkness out of the light? The question is a false one, since one without the other is unthinkable.

No more do we perceive the light than we do the darkness, but wherever they meet there is always conversation. We see this conversation between light and dark as colour. However, if we wish to experience each as they truly are we need to *think into being* the darkness alongside the light, since to our eyes alone darkness and light are quite invisible to us. Then if we do this we will find that each becomes a *being* in its own right. We experience them not simply as beings of absence. We experience them as beings of form and potential.

Chapter in a nutshell

- This chapter is in three parts.
- Firstly, we experience a candle flame radiating light out into the room where it stands, pushing back the darkness.
- Secondly, we experience the darkness in the room streaming in towards the candle flame, diluting the light.
- Thirdly, we consider how we are able to direct our thoughts towards a phenomenon such as darkness and experience it not as an absence of light but as a *being* in its own right equal to light.

8. Seeing the Unseeable in Clocks and Chairs

We sit in familiar surroundings on our favourite armchair. In front of us is an array of chairs arranged haphazardly around a table. They are unoccupied at the moment for we are alone. It is the end of a busy day and we are perfectly content simply to sit and rest a while, taking in the world as it comes.

All seems quiet until our eyes rest upon the clock which stands on the mantlepiece. The moment we see it we become aware of its constant tick-tock as its pendulum visibly swings back and forth. At first the clock itself conjures up many memories. Then what captures our attention is the pendulum's hypnotic swing and the sound of an onomatopoeic 'tick' as it goes one way and a slightly lower pitched 'tock' as it returns. Despite the tiredness of our body or perhaps even because of it, this synchronized combination of movement and sound begins to banish all our memories and associations with the clock by steadfastly maintaining our senses in the present moment.

Our body remains more or less still as we sit and listen. However, even though we, in terms of our body, are motionless, the world and our relationship to it are constantly on the move. Our situation is not unlike the experience we have of a landscape through the window of a moving train. There on a train, even though we remain seated and passive in our body, what we see through the window is constantly changing. We can think of it as constantly falling away. Trees, fields and houses momentarily enter our field of experience only to pass out of it again. Now, when we sit quietly in surroundings which do not move other than the motion of the clock, the difference is that it is we who bring movement to the world through our thoughts. It is the activity of our thinking in which one thought constantly replaces another which provides the motion for our ever-unfolding view of the world. Whenever we are awake, it is not the train which moves, but the *inner* train of our thoughts which carries us forward.

If we do not intend the activity of our thinking towards a particular object (be that a memory, a feeling or the world in general), this quality of ever-changing perspective is lost. Quite simply, to be aware of something is to be aware of it from the ever-changing perspective provided by the flow of our thoughts. If we are not aware of something, it is as if the train of consciousness comes to a standstill, all movement stops and we fall asleep to the object or the world. As long as one thought is being knocked off the pedestal of our awareness by another, we are awake to ourselves or the world or both. We experience this as a primal activity within us. Even if the world around us were to continue in a state so utterly unchanging that our sensory experience of it were perfectly uniform and constant,[1] so long as we remain active in our thinking, every moment of this otherwise uniform experience must still be transformed on a profound level. In our everyday language we call this transformation brought about by our activity of thought simply *time*, or *an awareness of time*.

Giving this experience a name, and a familiar one at that, does not even begin to explain how it comes about. As we behold the swinging pendulum, we know that the experience we have of its movement through time is bound up with our consciousness of the world. It poses the same questions to us as the rhythm of our breathing or the

movement of our limbs. Indeed, we maintain our sense of
being in the world through an awareness of time, certain in
our belief that yesterday happened, just as tomorrow will also
exist. We know that our tomorrows will become our todays,
just as our todays will inevitably become our yesterdays. We
live in the midst of our experience of time, and know that
this experience is hindered only by states of unconsciousness:
sleep, amnesia, coma, death. In fact, living in our body is to
live in and through time. And yet there is something universal in the continual swing of the pendulum and the way
that we are able to direct our consciousness towards it.

★   ★   ★

At first there seems no mystery.[2] We hear the ticking of the
clock and see its swinging pendulum. The pendulum swings
back and forth while the two hands move slowly around the
clock face. In this way we experience the clock in its
dimensions of space and time through our eyes and our ears,
and also, if we so wish, our sense of touch. Our hearing,
seeing and touching of the clock are real for us; but our
awareness that this is taking place is something yet more real.
The presence of the clock is mediated to us through our
various senses and the thoughts which come to meet them.
Awareness of our thoughts about the clock are mediated to us
through other thoughts. Considered this way, we have
greater certainty regarding our thoughts *about* the clock than
the clock itself. However, since our sensing of the clock and
our awareness that we are doing so coincide with one
another, we attribute certainty to what our senses provide for
us. Indeed, we build our whole sense of reality around this
coincidence, or concurrence, of sensing and being aware that
we are doing so.[3]

By contrast, the clock, though it marks out time, does so

without being aware of itself. Our eyes, ears and touch open us to the clock's presence but, like the clock, do so without an awareness of themselves. Devoid of awareness, our eyes and ears are open only to the present moment. They are not capable of retaining what has passed or of anticipating what might take place in the future. Our sense impressions are no more than a succession of events which have no connection with one another. The impressions we receive from the clock are continuous, and yet they lack the essential quality of continuity. A continuity of sensations alone does not account for an awareness of continuity.[4]

On these grounds alone, we are able to discern a discrepancy between what our eyes and ears sense of the moving pendulum and our self-aware experience of movement and sound. Though each swing of the pendulum, at least as far as our eyes and ears are concerned, is just the same, our experience of each swing is from an ever-changing perspective.[5] We then arrive at a notion of movement for the pendulum and unity for its accompanying sound even though what we perceive through our senses is no more than a succession of events with no relation to what has come before or what will happen next. These exist only in the present moment. They have no memory of what has just passed or any expectancy of what might happen in the future. To say, therefore, that each successive tick-tock and its concurrent swing of the pendulum is remembered and then built up into a picture with form and a sense of continuity is really no more than a half-truth. Remembering implies the remembrance of something, yet what brings form and continuity to our overall experience is not something which can ever be experienced purely through our senses in the first place. Continuity needs to come about from the side of thinking. Although one thought replaces another, just as one swing of the pendulum supersedes the previous one, our thinking retains a relationship with what has just passed, and is expectant of what might happen beyond the present moment. Thinking, in some manner or other, provides the continuity of experience which our senses alone can never provide.

At first the constant movement of the clock seems to raise more questions than can be answered at one time. So it is that we glance instead at some of the many static objects which surround us in the hope that they will be easier to comprehend. All of a sudden we have the possibility of directing our attention at a thousand different things, though in practice we are drawn by just a few: the chair we sit upon alongside our hands which rest upon it. Mingled with these are sensations associated with the weariness in our limbs, the smell from the kitchen and the expectancy of food, our day at work and our worries for tomorrow. In directing our attention at these things we know that we must overlook a thousand others. We do not see the spiders' webs in the corners of the ceiling, the dust on the skirting boards or the fingermarks on the walls and doors. We do not see any of these because we are not currently in a mind for housework. Nor do we see the books on the bookcase or the newspaper on the floor because we are not in a mind for reading. But that is not all. We also do not see every aspect or detail of the objects we *do* make ourselves aware of.

Just as we do not recognize all the objects in our surroundings (if we did, our every waking moment would present us with an unsustainable burden and we would be totally unable to live our lives), so too we do not recognize or individualize every detail in the objects we do intend our thoughts towards. We do not need to individualize every detail of a room to know that we are in a room. With a chair, we do not need to individualize every sense impression associated with it to know that it is a chair: every strand of fabric, every shading of grain in the wood or the underside we do not see. Similarly with a tree, we do not need to individualize every leaf, every bump or groove of the bark, or indeed every branch.[6] Our thoughts, therefore, are able to recognize things without taking note of their every detail.

Another observation we are able to make is that, as far as our eyes are concerned (as opposed to our thoughts), they see an object *only as long as they are open* and have a clear view of it.[7] Likewise, we must be within earshot of a sound to hear it, just as our body must come into contact with an object in order to touch and feel it. In short, our bodily organs are necessary for the world, in the form of sensations, to impress themselves upon our being. However, the concepts in all their many forms that enable us to order and recognize these sensations in the first place do not pass away when we close our eyes, move out of earshot or no longer touch something with our body. Everything which gives our sensations unity, relationship and meaning has the potential to live on within us after the initial sensory impressions are no longer there. This unifying dimension that enables us to recognize the object on the mantlepiece as a clock does not therefore pass with the present moment, but is able to live on within us without the need for the clock always to be present to our senses. In turn, this same unifying (conceptual) dimension in an individualized form enters the vocabulary of our thoughts and so enables us to recognize a picture of the same clock, draw a picture of it for ourselves or describe it to another person, or simply recall it as a memory. The world of concepts, though initially beckoned into consciousness by the offerings of the senses, is therefore by no means dependent upon it.

When we return our attention to the clock on the mantlepiece, we soon realize that we do not need to individualize all its details either to recognize it as the clock we know or to recognize it simply as a clock. For example, we might completely overlook the shape of the hands or the type of numerals used on the face, but still recognize the whole thing as a clock. Applying the same process to the swing of the pendulum (as opposed to the apparently static numerals on the clock's face), we are soon aware that each successive cycle of the pendulum is never there *all at once*. Similarly, the clock's sound is also never there *all at once*. Each tick-tock is a discrete event separated by a void we call silence. No tick ever sounds at the same time as a tock. In addition, the beginning of each sound is already passed when the ending of the same sound occurs. While to our senses the clock's face is ostensibly always there, what takes place with the *movement* of the pendulum is something quite different. As regards this and the recurrent sound of the clock's mechanism which accompanies it, these all involve a *closing of the senses* as a function of the object or event itself. Their unfolding to our physical sense organs is also accompanied by their disappearance.

Our eyes and ears receive a countless number of sense impressions from the moving pendulum and the sound which accompanies it, since at no point do we ever see more than an instantaneous phase during the pendulum's cycle or hear any more than a single instant of the clock's mechanism. However, it is also clear that we do not individualize every 'now-point' of this experience in order to recognize the movement of the pendulum or the sound which goes with it (just as we do not individualize every detail of the clock to know it is a clock, or the chair we are sitting on to recognize it as a chair). Furthermore, we are able to individualize both the sound and the movement even though they are never there all at once. Our unifying concepts, be they notions of movement or those which bring each successive tick followed by tock into relationship with one another, unfold while continually renewing themselves, rather than arriving all at once. This means we still individualize events such as this in the partial absence of the event itself. Therefore, strictly speaking, we should really say that we do not actually *see* the swing of the pendulum or *hear* its accompanying tick-tock at all. Rather, we must constitute it phase by phase, moment by moment.[8]

While all of this is taking place, each and every moment of our experience is coloured by the flow of thoughts which comes out to meet it. This flow of thoughts has its own self-sustaining unity made possible by the concurrence of experiencing and being aware that we are experiencing. Awareness of our bringing forth of thoughts (our activity of thinking) also gives us a constant connection with what has just passed. We not only bring continuity to our sensations, but are able to become self-aware that we are doing so. It is this flow of consciousness which spans what our senses mediate to us, giving our sense impressions, such as those we receive from the swinging pendulum, something they can never attain themselves: continuity. We call this state of spanning what our senses offer us an awareness of time.[9] It is the mystery by which we acquire not only our awareness of time, but also the freedom to be bored or interested, or for time to pass quickly or slowly.

By living in the midst of the flow of consciousness, something else is made possible. Through reflecting on the activity of our thinking, we create a bridge between the immediate past and the present moment. The activity of our thinking precedes the content of thought. Through thinking the activity of our thinking, we also find the one point of certainty within the total spectrum of our existence. Our own activity as thinking beings becomes the content of our thoughts. Yet the reflective capacity by which we find this most intimate reality within us is also the capacity which endows us with temporal awareness. Through this two-sided activity, time and consciousness come together as one. The point of certainty we are capable of finding within ourselves is therefore not static; it is a moving locus which defines both the certainty of our existence and the continuity of our being through time. Certainty about our own existence is the prerequisite for our experience of time, just as an awareness of the temporal flow of our thoughts is the means by which we maintain certainty about our own existence in the world.

★   ★   ★

With this in mind we turn our attention back to the chairs arranged unevenly around the table in front of us. As soon as we do so, we are no longer aware of the presence of the clock. It could quite easily stop ticking and we would not be conscious of it. The chairs, meanwhile, fully engage our thoughts. They are each of a slightly different design, though of similar height and size and so fit neatly around the table. A couple of them have upholstered seats, one has a wicker seat while the others are just plain wood with a cushion resting on them. The fact that they are arranged around a table means that we see each one from a different angle. Some we see from behind, a couple from the side, while we cannot really say that we see the remainder from the front since they are mostly obscured by the table and the other chairs. They inhabit their own place within the room such that the sensory impressions we receive from each chair are very different. It is clear to us that in no way do we see all of the chairs together. What our eyes see of them is at best dispersed and disjointed.

We already know that we do not need to make ourselves aware of every detail of the chairs to know that they are chairs. We overlook the dents and scratches in the varnish even though some of them are clearly visible to us. We also know that it is impossible for us ever to see any one of the chairs *all at once*, since we can never see a chair's underside at the same time as its top, its back as well as its front. In this sense we begin to see the similarities between the chairs and the movement of the pendulum in that neither can we ever see all at once: one because of *space*, the other because of *time*. Thus, as with the swing of the pendulum and the sound which accompanies it, we are able to arrive at a unified experience of a chair in the partial absence of the object itself.

When we focus our attention upon the chairs, the most immediate reality for us is always of a conceptual nature. It is something revealed to us directly through the activity of our thinking. We cannot deny to ourselves that we also experience them as something out there in the world as things which make their presence known through our senses. As such, we experience them both as something detached from us and as something that is revealed to us from within our thoughts. Undoubtedly they are something beyond the bounds of our body. We can sit on them and they support our weight. We know them to be real in themselves and waiting to be recognized. And yet the very fact of our awareness and subsequent cognizance of them forces us to ask what aspect of the chairs exists *beyond* us, and what aspect of the chairs exists *within* us.

Though we are fully aware of the chairs, we might say that a great many aspects of what we suppose to be the source of our experience of them are unknown to us. For example, the

inner nature of the substance from which they are made, the
nature of the light by which we see them, the workings of
our eyes, along with countless other factors, are to begin with
all a mystery to us. What we do know is that if we close our
eyes we no longer see the chairs. Similarly, if there is no light
in the room we also will not see them. However, all this tells
us is that our eyes are a precondition for seeing the chairs and
not the cause; and that the light is also a precondition for
seeing the chairs and not the cause. A window is a precondition for sunlight to come into a room, but is not the
cause of the light. The window will influence the light,
perhaps colouring it or giving it certain inflections; but it is no
more the cause of the light than our eyes and the light to
which they are open are the cause of the chair. Our senses
will colour the world, and give it inflections and emphasis.
They may also blot out a whole aspect of the world if, for
example, they are weak, damaged or in some way covered
over. But this does not diminish our sense of reality. It simply
alters the emphasis with which we form our pictures of the
world.[10] Human reality is essentially a conceptual one, not a
sense-perceived one. Indeed, that which enables us to
recognize each chair, object or event around us is not
something which is perceived through the senses. Rather, the
senses are a pre-condition for the world of substance to come
to our awareness, and not the cause, since over and above *all*
sense experience human thinking shows itself to be pre-
endowed to enable the experience of form and relation *in the
sense world*. The conceptual world of thinking is not only
regulative, but also constitutive of the sense world.

This notwithstanding, though we recognize the chairs
through our activity of thinking, and not the activity of our
senses, we cannot escape the notion that they are something
external to us. Our thoughts do not *see* a chair in terms of its

substance, just as they do not *recognize* it in terms of its substance either. Rather, they reach out to something which is
beyond the substance of the specific object. Specifically, we
might describe what our thinking perceives as a para-sensible
dimension to sense perception.

Through an activity of perceiving which is intended in the
same direction as our physical sense organs, but which is not
an activity of perceiving in any conventional sense, our
thinking reaches *between and beyond* what our senses alone
mediate to us. But our thinking can achieve this only by
reaching out to something which is of the same nature as
itself. Our thoughts are of a conceptual nature; but also every
chair, when considered in terms of what exists between and
beyond what our senses see of it, is itself *pure relation*. Each
chair before us is unique. A chair, and likewise every object
and event in the world, may be considered the embodiment
of a specific conceptual nature in so far as, behind its
appearance to our senses, there exists a condition of pure
relation. This conceptual aspect is not universal, but specific.
For each of the chairs before us there is a unique concept
inherent to it. Every *inherent concept* embodies a different form
of chairness. This concept is not accessible through our
senses. Rather, since it is of a like nature to our own thoughts,
our thinking, as a sense organ in its own right, perceives it
directly.

Inherent concepts are the medium through which our
thoughts have a dialogue with the perceptible world. In the
case of the inherent concepts relating to each of the chairs
before us, they are individual entities embodying the
relationships inherent in each specific object. They are the
beings behind and beyond the physical appearance of the
chairs. As such, they are different from the universal concepts
from which our thoughts are spun. These are individualized

in the act of recognition. Inherent concepts, by contrast, cannot be individualized since they are already individual entities. As part of the act of recognition, they must undergo a quite different process of transformation.

The act of recognizing the chairs in front of us is itself a unique event. It sets in train a play of concepts involving the universal concept chair *beyond* us and the concepts inherent in the chairs *before* us. Like an event in the physical world, this play of concepts leaves a footprint. As our thoughts are intended towards the fragmentary experience of the chairs we receive through our senses, we individualize the universal concept chair slightly differently for each chair, thereby bringing unity to the sensory plurality placed before us. But what makes the process of intending our thoughts towards the world possible in the first place is that they are reaching out to something of like nature to themselves. It is through a process of *like reaching out to like* that we are able to intend our thoughts towards the inherent concepts of the chairs. In so doing, in a manner of speaking, the inherent concept of each intended object also comes out to meet us. We might say that it is released, since through our act of becoming aware of any one of the chairs it thereby finds its conceptual connection first with the other chairs, then all chairs, and subsequently with the rest of the total world existence in a conceptual form. Thus, by intending our thinking towards them, they are released from the particular objects to which they, until that moment, had been bound. In the vocabulary of cognitive science, through acts of recognition, each inherent concept towards which our consciousness is intended is *universalized*

In the light of this it is possible to say that the mission of the human faculty of cognition is to unify these two elements of reality: the conceptual which permeates every object and happening in the world with the conceptual as manifest in thinking.[11] In this way, human thinking shows itself to be something which not only brings unity to the sense world, but which also elevates the conceptual between and beyond the sense world such that it is brought into unity with the conceptual world in its totality. Specifically, when we cognize any object or event, we instigate a real change in the fundamental structure of the world. Human thinking, therefore, is a primal force in the world.

★ ★ ★

When we turn our attention away from the chairs and back to the clock, we immediately become aware of its ticking sound just as we lose awareness of the chairs. We notice first that the hands have moved since we last looked at them. The pendulum, too, continues to swing back and forth. Our eyes are open to what carries impressions of the swinging pendulum to us, namely, the light. If there were no light, we would not see the pendulum. Similarly, our ears are sensitive to what carries the sound to us, namely, the subtle changes in the air. If there were no air, we would not hear its tick-tock. But the pendulum and the sound of the clock are just the sensory appearance of beings in their own right. These beings (what we have also called inherent concepts) are what our thoughts perceive directly. That we are not aware of them in our everyday state of consciousness is the result of two fundamental dispositions of mind.

The first is that our thoughts are usually dominated by the sensory appearance of things. The result of this is that we ordinarily understand experience to be something that is 'sense-filled'. However, we can begin to challenge this notion by paying particular attention to the qualities of relationship inherent in phenomena such as darkness, silence and empty spaces, or of phenomena of absence generally. The second is that we are not accustomed to intending our thinking towards things which are apparently beyond our own being but which again have no sensory content. The result of this, just as it is in the sense world, is that if we do not intend our thinking towards something or other, it will simply pass us by. The way we can begin to overcome this is by paying special attention to the fact that we must think the chair before us in order to become aware of it; we must think the ticking of the clock in order to hear it; when driving we must think the pedestrian who is crossing the road in front of us or we may not see them, or when we are crossing the road we must think the approaching car or we may not see it. In the case of the inherent concept or being of an object, that too needs to be thought in order that we may become aware of it. But either we do not know that such a thing exists or we do not know what we are looking for. That we do not think the inherent concept is therefore largely a matter of habit; and we are no more coloured by habit than in our thoughts. For example, on a walk in the country, the botanist may take note of all the flowers while his or her companions see none of them; the ornithologist may notice all the birdsong while his or her companions hear none of it; the person from the city may perhaps notice how beautiful it all is, or only how cold and muddy it is, while his or her companions, who are used to it, will think nothing of it. The difference with the conceptual world is that, rather than certain aspects of the sense world passing us by, a whole other dimension of reality is being overlooked.

The example of objects in motion (such as the swinging pendulum) can be of special help to us because their recognition makes more transparent what ordinarily happens when we recognize *any* object. For our eyes and ears, each swing of the pendulum is never there all at once; but the very fact that what our senses perceive is constantly falling away gives us an opportunity for the conceptual dimension of this happening to come to the fore. Yet this must happen for all objects, since it is the falling away of what is perceptually disparate which allows our thoughts to perceive what lies beyond the senses and so accomplish acts of recognition in the first place. Each chair in front of us is different in so far as what our eyes see of them, but we still group them together as chairs. That is, we recognize them as chairs despite the fact that they all look different and our view of them is fragmentary. What this means is that, in order for us to recognize them each as chairs, our thinking needs to reach beyond their sense-perceptible form. However, in the case of the moving pendulum, the flight of a bird or the path of a shooting star, this takes place as a function of the object itself. The sense-perceptible appearance recedes of its own accord. Then, when we are aware of what it is that exists beyond this sense-perceptible appearance, that is to say what remains once everything on a sense-perceptible level has fallen away, we will be able to make more conscious for ourselves what we have called here the inherent concept.

When we are more accustomed to thinking what lies beyond the sense perceptible in the case of objects in movement, we will begin to *see* with ever greater clarity the unseeable dimension to the chairs before us, just as we can *see* the unperceivable nothingness of darkness in the light of a candle or the imperceptible connections between stars in the night sky.

★   ★   ★

Recognition is not an act of seeing or of hearing, but of *overcoming* what is seen and heard through our physical senses.

When we are confronted by something we are unable to recognize, we realize how recognition is also about striving for balance. For example, if we are faced with something we cannot recognize despite our conscious efforts, a feeling of imbalance or tension exists until that situation is resolved. This is something we can observe directly from within ourselves. Beyond this, we may also observe from within ourselves that just as recognition is about balance, so too it is also a matter of symmetry. This symmetry exists in the way that two conceptual polarities are unified in the moment of cognition. As a universal concept is individualized from out of the total existence in a universalized form, so the inherent concept towards which our consciousness is intended is universalized from out of the perceptible world fabric. What is conceptually universal becomes specific; what is conceptually unique is given a universalized form. Only in this meeting of the conceptual in thinking with the conceptual which permeates the world do we truly attain cognitive balance.

We, as human beings, achieve this balance alongside an awareness of ourselves as individuals. We not only recognize the world, but are aware that we are doing so. The central point of this activity of self-awareness has a name. We call it our I. I-ness is the motive power of our thinking by which we become self-aware. As an activity, it is disposed towards bringing together the conceptual in the world with the conceptual in thinking.

The nature of I-ness is to strive for cognitive resolution and balance, the result of which is consciousness itself.

Our I lives out of, and therefore in the midst of, our activity of thinking. It exits in the selfsame point where we find certainty for our own being by making the activity of our thinking the content of our thoughts. This self-validating activity then becomes a tangible force in the sense-perceptible world. Through the act of intentionality, we project this activity out into the world at large.

Consciousness is the projecting of our I into the world.

By thinking the activity of our own thinking, our I is not just projected inwards towards itself. By intending the activity of our I towards our own thoughts, we become aware of ourselves; by intending the activity of our I towards its own activity, we find a point of certainty within ourselves. Yet the wonder of our power of intentionality is that through it our I also projects the reality that exists in our thinking activity out into the world.

Intentionality is the projection of our I-ness out into the world.

The more we live within the interplay defined by the above maxims, the more we will find meaning in the words: *through understanding ourselves we can begin to understand the world; through understanding the world we can begin to understand ourselves.*

We are open to the wonders of the world, while in return, we bestow something which only we as self-aware beings can give. What we give to the world are unity, form and relationship in space and beyond space, in time and beyond time. For as well as being that aspect of our existence which provides the impetus for our reflective capacity, it is the I's predisposition to self-awareness which enables us to bestow to all evolving world phenomena the dimension of passing time.

The being of time is itself the ability of our I to be aware of itself, and to project that being into the world.

*   *   *

The world breathes into us through our senses, while we breathe out a parallel conceptual world to meet it with our thoughts. In this way, by directing our I towards it, the sense world undergoes a change. This conceptual breath which is directed by our I consists of the conceptual world as individualized by the activity of our thinking. At the very same moment, the conceptual beings which lie behind the sense world are released by human thinking. In their release they become universal, thereby finding their place in the world: chairs with all other chairs, constellations with all other constellations, trees with all other trees. Thus, by thinking into unity, form and relationship the objects and events of the sense world, the conceptual world which permeates all things is brought into relationship with the conceptual world in its totality.

Through our acts of recognition we do not just complete the reality of the world, but affect the conceptual structure that underpins it. This has no greater bearing upon the world than when suddenly the door opens and in walks another human being. Their presence completely fills our attention, for instead of looking at them with our eyes and listening to them with our ears, we see and hear them directly with our thoughts. In so doing, our own being momentarily appears to step aside, just as it does when we are asleep. In its place, the being of this other person is able to present itself to us as we would know ourselves. Though we see and hear them with our eyes and ears, we know that through these senses we do not really see or hear this person as they truly are. But in the very moment that we observe them directly with our thinking, we know that we have taken the act of recognition to a deeper level.

★   ★   ★

As an exercise, we try to make ourselves aware of something obvious in our surroundings which we simply did not notice because we did not direct our thinking towards it. Just as we are leaving a room in which we have spent some time, we stop for a moment in the doorway, turn around, and try to notice something to which our senses were open, but which our thoughts were not receptive to because they were otherwise engaged. It might be the scent of the room which completely passed us by. There might be flowers on the table we did not see; there might be something special about the colour or fabric of the curtains; the furniture may have been arranged in a particular way to make us feel welcome; there may have been pictures or photographs in the room which for some reason did not catch our eye.

In recognizing something of this nature, we bring to life the fact that we need to think the world into being in order to become aware of it. Then, in the moment that we do this, we begin to observe purely with our thoughts what we otherwise overlooked. We do this by recognizing what it is in the object of our attention which is of a like nature to our thoughts.

To help us do this, we imagine the being of an object as the totality of what is left once everything of a physical nature has been abstracted away. The nature of this being is one of pure relationship, pure form, pure unity; it is everything but appearance. When we feel the likeness between our thoughts and what lies beyond the sensory appearance of things we will also experience how our thoughts are able to reach out and touch the world. For what they touch is as real to the world of thinking as the world of substance is real to our outstretched limbs.

Chapter in a nutshell

- We contemplate the difference between a static object, such as a chair, and an object in movement, such as a swinging pendulum or the sound that a clock makes.
- An object's movement is transitory. It is never there all at once and is continually falling into the past.
- Our thinking comprehends such an object as a unity by

reaching out to the concept that embraces the specific object or event in its wholeness. This concept exists over and above the object as it presents itself to our senses and is called the *inherent concept*.

- This chapter considers how human consciousness brings this inherent concept together with a universal concept, and in so doing becomes a real and active force in the world.

- It also looks at how our sense of self or I is the central point of this activity, endowing us with an awareness of continuity and therefore of time.

9. Listening to the Rain[12]

There is nothing quite like sitting indoors in comfortable surroundings when outside heavy rain is falling. We can watch it as it strikes the windows, flowing down in rivulets which pattern the glass. We can listen to it not just as it sweeps across the window panes but also as it drums on the roof above our heads or upon the road and pavements outside. We see it too as it falls in waves sculpted by the wind, fluttering the leaves on the trees and whipping the puddles into beautiful shapes which last no more than an instant. Then when the wind ceases we notice how the rain appears strangely still as it descends in vertical shafts of grey, bouncing once as it hits the ground before finally flowing away into the earth.

When we open one of the windows, our whole experience of the rain becomes more immediate. We feel a freshening breeze on our face and take in the rain's purifying smell. But the effect of this smell far from drawing us into the moment instead takes us back to the past by conjuring up in us all sorts of memories. The rain causes us to reminisce upon our past, perhaps upon a walk or picnic cut short by an unexpected change in the weather, a favourite raincoat, a hat or an umbrella. It calls up these images before our mind's eye with surprising vividness. And when these memories fade from our attention they are superseded by others. Meanwhile, each and every memory that we have is coloured by so rich a palette of emotions from happy through to sad that after a while we are scarcely conscious of the rain at all.

When finally our memories step aside and we are back in the present, we find that our emotions are no less active. On the one hand we are pleased that it is raining because the garden had become so dry that all the plants were withering. A good soaking of rain was just what they needed. At the same time, we are annoyed both at the rain and ourselves because we have washing we wish to hang outside to dry. As we look at the basketful of damp washing, we cannot hide our frustration at the fact that it is raining.

The rain, therefore, is the object of a mix of sometimes contradictory emotions. It also affects us in a way that helps to consolidate our sense of belonging in the world. It is a spur for a whole host of personal reminiscences and also brings us both pleasure and frustration. All of this is special and particular to us. No one else has the same memories and emotions regarding the rain as we do. What is more, the picture we have of the rain within ourselves is one that only we can have. Not only do we see, feel and hear the rain from a unique point in space that only we can inhabit, but the sharpness of our eyes, our sensitivity to warmth and cold, the clarity of our hearing and countless other factors all affect the final picture we have of the rain in terms of how it looks, how it feels and what it sounds like. In the very same moment that we are experiencing the rain, others are also doing so, but in completely different ways. Their memories, their associations, their feelings, their inner picture of the rain must inevitably be different from ours.

All the while the rain continues to fall. It will continue whether we are there to look at it or not. We can go outside and let it run down our face, or jump up and down while waving our arms about. It seems that whatever we do it will still follow its own laws, its own rhythms, its own way. We may suppose that it would still be raining had we died yesterday, or last week, or even had we never been born at all. It continues quite independently of us. But not so our memories or the feelings we have towards it. These are entirely dependent upon us for their existence. They shift and change with our moods, our fancies, our thoughts as they lead from one thing to another. If we were not there, if we had died yesterday or last week, or if we had never even been born at all, the world of feelings, memories and pictures we now experience within ourselves would not exist. This inner world of experience which is unique to us is something we are able to call our *soul*. As such, our own individual life of soul is dependent upon us for its very existence.

What the rain is for us lives within our soul. But there are other people who also see and recognize the rain. They cannot see the world as we do since they do not have our eyes, our ears, our sense of touch. Nor do they have our memories and associations, our likes and dislikes. Yet they share the same world as us. They live in the same moment as us and are able to see and hear the rain falling outside their own homes. Perhaps they call it rain; perhaps they call it by some other word. They view it from their perspective, that is from their own world of soul. But what they recognize in the rain, beyond the word they use to describe it, beyond the feelings they have towards it, beyond the appearance of the rain to their bodily organs, beyond the picture of the rain they have in their soul, is what we are able to call the *spirit* of the rain.

The spirit of the rain is what exists as a being between and beyond the picture we have of it to our senses. The rain would continue to fall whether we were there to watch it or not. What it is in itself exists in a dimension of being which is beyond our soul. It is something independent of our own being, and yet the laws, the rhythms and the way of the rain are not just there for us to recognize. These are ever present and there for all people. The spirit which is active in the world is also active in thinking generally. Through thinking the rain we all therefore touch something of the spirit of the rain. It is given to us through cognition and recognition. It lives in the activity of our thinking through which the world reveals itself to us. At first we do not see the spirit of the rain as it is active in our thoughts. We see only its action upon our body and soul as the spirit is distilled into a picture of the rain within us. The spirit of the rain is active behind and beyond this picture; yet this picture is but an appearance of the rain. As a picture it lives within our soul; it is special to us. Our soul takes hold of it and makes it its own. But to see the spirit of the rain active within us we must think the activity of our thinking. For only there is the spirit active in a form which has meaning in itself, and not simply meaning for us.

★　★　★

Within our soul, we live in one moment which is forever superseded by the next. We can relive our memories again and again, just as we are able to live in the midst of familiar emotions. A memory can bring us happiness on one occasion, sadness on another. An emotion that feels appropriate in one setting may be abhorrent in another. Our soul is in continual change. But within it there exists a point of constancy which we carry from one instant to the next, from one minute to the next, from one day to the next. This point of constancy within our soul is our *I*. It is the fulcrum through which we live our thoughts, memories and emotions.

Our I lies both within and beyond our soul since it is also the point of activity through which we become aware of the existence of our soul. It lives in the midst of our soul but is also a point from which we are able to look into our soul. Similarly, our I lies both within and beyond space and time, since it is also the point of activity through which we become aware of the nature of space and time. Not only does our I move through space and time, it helps to form space and time as it goes. But in doing so it projects our qualities of soul out into these dimensions. The emotions of joy and frustration we have for the rain are events in the world like the rain itself. Our I is the bringer of unity and relationship between these events. Through bringing together the spirit of the rain as it lives in our thinking with the contents of our soul which we bring forth in relation to the sense impressions of the rain, we create a spiritual bond between our life of soul and the physical and spiritual unfolding of the world. This new creation, which is formed in strict accordance with our thoughts and feelings for everything around us, is really a bridge between the sense world, the world of soul and the world of spirit. For although it is of a purely immaterial nature, it is as real as any bridge in the physical world, and also as permanent. As such, cognition itself becomes a moral activity with the power both to heal or to poison, since it leaves in its wake a spiritual trail which is a direct consequence of how our soul life is disposed towards the world. This trail is what we as individuals of body, soul and spirit offer the world as a gift each and every moment of our conscious waking lives.

Chapter in a nutshell

- We experience rain and form an individual picture of it.
- The rain also conjures up in us memories along with emotions such as pleasure and frustration. These are all unique to us and so belong to our *soul*.
- Meanwhile, the *spirit* of the rain is what exists beyond our individual experience but which is accessible to all people.
- While our soul is in a continual state of change through its

pictures, emotions and memories, there is also a point of constancy within it. This is our *I*.

- As well as introducing notions of soul and spirit, this chapter considers our I as a central point of activity bridging the three worlds of sense, soul and spirit.

Part IV:

THINKING OUR FEELINGS
AND MEMORIES

10. The Compost Heap

At the end of the garden there is a compost heap. It is in a corner beside a wall on one side and a ramshackle fence on the other. Behind the wall is a footpath, and beyond that a road; while behind the fence is another garden. Despite the fact that it is no higher than our waist, the compost heap itself is made up of substance from across the globe. There are coffee grounds from Kenya, banana skins from Ecuador, kiwi skins from New Zealand, apple cores from France and tea bags containing tea from India. There are also the tops and tails of beans grown in the garden no more than a few paces away, and the peelings of local potatoes bought from a market just down the road. So it is that the object now before us extends in ever wider circles until it encompasses the whole world.

As well as spanning the earth through its substance, the compost heap also embodies many other dimensions. For example, it is a world of colour where the dark outer leaves of a purple cabbage are squashed up against the brilliant oranges from the skins of clementines, satsumas and tangerines. While all around, countless shades of green and brown dominate the pyramidal heap. Then right on top, crowning this multi-coloured and multinational edifice, lies a drooping bunch of cut flowers with green gelatinous stems at one end and fading white, red, yellow and blue blossoms at the other.

The heap is also a world of smells which exists alongside the parallel worlds of moisture and warmth. Indeed, in this corner of the garden there is such a mixture of smells that we sometimes find it difficult to place any one of them amongst our memories. The impressions we receive remind us of late autumn, of walking along tree-lined paths ankle deep with clinging leaves; but also they make us think of dampness, of the earth, of simply being outdoors.

As we come nearer we picture ourselves reaching out and touching the heap with our hands. In the end we think better of it, since from close up it looks such an unpredictable mass of things that we are happy to leave the feel of it to our imagination. For most of all, the compost heap embodies the worlds of growing and decaying. Below the flowers crawl the many insects which inhabit this place. At first we see only the earwigs and scuttling woodlice as they move about the surface of the heap. What takes place beneath, at least for the moment, is a mystery to us. But without further ado we roll up our sleeves, take in our hands the pitchfork which stands in the ground nearby and thrust it into the centre of the pile. Only when it is fully embedded do we then lift with all the strength in our arms at the same time as twisting the pitchfork with our wrists. The flowers fall to one side as the insects scatter in all directions. What we reveal is a contracting life of sorts where the loose bucketfuls of waste which characterize the outside of the heap have gradually shrunk into a form of darkened matter.

Some of what we see is still recognizable. The fragile halves of eggshells remain alongside peach stones, plum stones and avocado skins skewered by broken twigs and fibres. There is even a rusting nail. The rest is just a crumbling mass of forming earth riddled with worms. There are small red worms which knot themselves together in tight clusters. The others are large and pink in colour, and immediately begin to concertina their solitary way back into the gloom from which they have been disturbed. But also amidst the worms and dark shrinking earth we see the white roots and budding shoots of discarded green potatoes. Then beside these we notice that some of the green stems protruding from the heap are not the sliced up offcuts from the kitchen, but the beginnings of tomato plants emerging from their tiny seeds. Altogether, through its processes of unfolding and contracting, it is as if the compost heap were slowly breathing in and out.

★ ★ ★

This process of breathing happens in a place which is open to the elements: to the rain, the sun, the moon and the stars. It is also open to the air and the wind and what the wind carries with it. Car fumes are mixed with the scent of flowers; dust hovers alongside the buzz of insects; seeds and pollen fly with the wind alongside the flight of birds. Visibly or invisibly, these all touch the compost heap at our feet. But also carried upon the wind are featherlight sweet wrappers and airy crisp packets which are whipped up from the footpath and road just beyond. Some inevitably find their way onto the compost heap where they are soon covered by leaves and fresh bucketfuls of waste from the kitchen.

When the time comes to prize open this living mass of substance, despite their silky delicacy and transparent lightness, the occasional sweet wrapper and crisp packet is revealed largely intact. Waiting in the writhing darkness while squashed between layers of growth and decay, some of their silvery interiors are now a little tarnished and a few of them have been ripped into straggly pieces. However, their colourful logos, their lists of ingredients, their black-and-white bar-codes are all still legible beneath the encrusted dirt. And when we touch them with our pitchfork they do not crumble away. Rather, it appears that they do not really participate in the processes of either growth or decay taking place all around them.

And yet, apart from the insects, simply by looking at the diverse ingredients of the compost heap we cannot really distinguish between what is in a state of growth, what is in a state of decay, and what to all intents and purposes is lifeless. We know that the plastic wrappers do not look as fresh and shiny as they undoubtedly did when they were new, and so must be undergoing a transformation of sorts. But we cannot claim to see it. Similarly, in the short time that we are there, the tomato plants do not grow or the potatoes sprout. Nor do we see the tea bags disintegrate, the cut flowers drop their petals, the banana skins turn black or the nail become rusty any more than they have done already. Nor is it simply a question of what moves and what is static. The lanky stems of the tomato plants sway in the breeze and move with their surroundings; but so do the plastic wrappers as they unfold and crinkle of their own accord.

★   ★   ★

We can observe the heap in many different ways. For example, if we allow our thoughts about the compost heap to take on a life of their own, we begin to see what lies beyond the substance from which it is made. By this means we are able to observe every aspect of the compost heap *as process*. We experience all of this; but on its own, our thinking is not enough. Our thoughts about the world at large live within us. In addition, these thoughts live alongside other thoughts concerning our own state of being. But the foundations of our being are themselves growth and decay, expansion and contraction, unfolding and withering, living and dying. The rhythms inherent in these processes are the ones that underpin our own inner life. That is, they bestow qualities upon our thoughts about the rest of existence. They colour our relationship with everything outside our thoughts. These qualities, these colourations, are our *feelings*.

As soon as the processes taking place within the compost heap enter our thoughts, they inevitably mingle with our feelings. But this is necessary since in order for the world to have meaning for us we must experience it in relation to something. Our feeling life provides this. We differentiate between the unfolding and contracting of the world through our life of feeling. We feel them in relation to the rhythms of growth and decay which we experience within ourselves. Our feelings provide the reference points against which, through the measures of flow and resistance, we relate to the outer processes of the world.

By bringing together the life of the world with the life of our own being, we are able to feel the veracity (or indeed the falseness) of our individual thoughts. While our thoughts penetrate our feelings and our feelings penetrate our thoughts, our I projects what lives within us through our faculty of intentionality. Thus, when we direct our thinking towards the compost heap, we experience how our inner life resonates (or not) with what it is intended towards.

When we experience the processes of growth or decay taking place within the compost heap, they have the potential to resonate within us. For when we experience this resonance where our thought life and feeling life come together, each supporting the other, we see the different processes of life as perceptions in their own right. Our perceptions of the world then appear cocooned within the qualities and colourations that underpin our own existence. We quite literally *see* the life within and around the dormant plum stones as well as within and around the decomposing vegetable matter. We thereby *see* whether they are tending towards life or death, growth or decay, unfolding or contracting. And when we look towards the discarded sweet wrappers and crisp packets and *see* no glow of growth or decay, we recognize that they are something quite different from their surroundings. For even around the rusting nail and the stones on the ground we have an inkling of a very ancient sort of life which echoes right the way through the world-wide substance before us.

Chapter in a nutshell

- A compost heap embodies processes of both decay and growth.
- When we reveal what lies beneath its surface we see writhing worms, decaying matter and sprouting shoots. We also see sweet wrappers. These appear not to participate in the same way with the life processes going on around them.
- We then endeavour to observe the processes taking place in the heap directly with our thoughts in conjunction with the rhythms and fluctuations of our own existence, that is in relation to our *feelings*.
- This chapter considers how we can begin to use our faculties of thinking and feeling as organs of perception capable of experiencing the processes of the world as beings in their own right.

11. Reading Our Feelings and Remembering Our Thoughts

Looking upon a bookcase filled with books is itself like the picture we have of our own soul.

When we experience a bookcase through our eyes and other senses we at first experience only the surface of the books and the shelves that support them. We see the different shapes of the books, their colours and their various heights and widths. We also see what is written upon their spines, but not on their front and back covers, and least of all what is printed upon their pages. Thus we acknowledge that our initial experience is a very superficial one. In order to step beyond this surface appearance of the bookcase and discover what lies behind the spines and titles of the books we see there, we must select an individual volume and open it up.

So it is with the inner life of our own thoughts, even if we are not at first aware of it. When we intend our thinking towards something, ordinarily what this means is that we then experience it as a so-called *mental picture*.[1] For example, we direct our attention towards the bookcase. What our thoughts working together with our senses deliver of the bookcase appears at first not to be the full reality of the object, but just a superficial picture of it. The picture nature of this experience becomes still more evident to us when we close our senses (for example our eyes) but still retain an image of the bookcase within us. The fact that the picture is retained means that it is in some way a product of our own thoughts. Meanwhile, when we open our eyes again, the picture nature of our experience continues. The difference is that our mental pictures have certain attributes which cause us to situate the world they are representing beyond the bounds of our physical body. Thus, we experience the bookcase as an object *outside* ourselves through a mental picture that arises *within* us.

However, while directing our attention to the bookcase and its many unopened volumes we can also come to the realization that the mental pictures we do have of the world within us are also prone to half-truths and falsehoods. To begin with, since we can only see their spines as they sit upon the shelves of the bookcase (and not their pages), we cannot really tell if they are books at all. The rows of leather-bound classics may in fact be the cleverly concealed doors to a drinks cabinet, or they may be boxes disguised as books. And even if they are all books, we can still be deceived. As a result of some curious mishap at the printers, all the pages may be blank. On the other hand, some mischievous person may have swapped over the dust jackets between all the hardbacks so that they are no longer what they say they are. All of this goes to show that the mental picture we form of the bookcase may not correspond with the reality behind the surface.

At first it seems that we can verify what our senses offer us only through closer and closer scrutiny of the sense world: we need to scrape the surface of the bookcase to see and feel whether it is made of solid wood or is just veneered; we must leaf through the pages of a book to see what is written upon them, and so on. In each case, we are driven to seek more sensory information. However, in doing so, we can never escape the fact that, without our thoughts, all that flows upon us through our senses remains formless and without meaning. The inescapable fact of thinking's engagement with the world is that it forms mental pictures regardless of how detailed our examination of the sense world is. Then so long as our mental pictures remain a mystery, whatever these mental pictures are a representation of must also remain a mystery to us.

These limitations reach right to the core of our existence such that for much of the time we are little more than an appearance even to ourselves. The rumblings in our stomach when we are hungry, as well as hunger itself, the in-and-out of our breathing, as well as the rhythm which goes with it, the pins and needles in our legs or the cold in our toes, as well as the fact that we have legs and toes, are observed through the body's own inwardly directed sense organs, namely, the nervous system. As with our sense organs that are directed out into the world, those that are internal to us also require us to intend our thinking through them. For example, we need to intend our thinking towards our stomach, our breathing and our limbs in order to become aware of them; and if there is a break in our nervous system, or it is damaged in some way, we will lose touch with them just as we lose sight of the world if our eyes are closed or damaged. But the result of directing our thinking towards those aspects of ourselves we might otherwise consider to be within us is still a mental picture. Therefore, in terms of our thinking's tendency to form mental pictures, both the essence of the world and the nature of our existence in that world are lost in their transformation into pictures within us, just as the life of a landscape dies upon the chemical changes in photographic film or within the digitized memory of a camera.

How can we begin to understanding how this affects us in a practical way? Once again, our experience of the bookcase and its many closed volumes can help us in this regard. It tells us that forming a mental picture of a so-called object does not guarantee that the 'intended object', however strongly or faintly it presents itself to our consciousness, has been recognized correctly or indeed that it exists at all.

As we have already noted, some of the apparent books upon the bookcase may not be books at all but leather panelling or boxes made to look like books. Similarly, the bookcase may appear to be made of wood when really it is just chipboard with a plastic wood-effect veneer. However, another of the problems we must confront when we live too much within our mental pictures is the possibility that we are capable of projecting into being something which isn't really there. This applies to objects themselves as much as to the relationships between them. Thus, it is perfectly possible for us to form a mental picture of a particular book upon one of the shelves when in reality that book is not there at all.

For example, *in extremis*, perhaps if the light in the room where the bookcase stands is weak, or there are strong shadows being cast upon it, we might single out a particular book we are looking for; but on closer inspection we find that where we believed the book to be there is nothing other than an empty book-shaped space. We somehow convinced ourselves that we saw something, when really all that was there was an empty space from where we then surmise another book had probably been removed.[2] Similarly, we might be looking for a particular book when, for a moment, we believe we see it; but it later turns out to be another book entirely. On the other hand, through the dominant role played by mental pictures in our awareness of things, it is also possible for us to become aware of something we simply cannot recognize or find a context for. We form a mental picture of it even though we do not know what it is. For example, we might look across to the bookcase and clearly see something yellow upon one of the shelves, but be unable to recognize what it is. The fact that we have become aware of it means that we have intended our thinking towards it and individualized it from out of its surroundings into a mental picture of some sort; but we have done so on the basis that it is something as yet unknown to us. Such acts of cognition usually resolve themselves, and the object without a context or within a false context turns out to be nothing more sinister than a misplaced packet of sweets, a yellow duster folded in an unexpected way or a stack of old birthday cards.

Through such instances as these it is clear that to form a mental picture of something is an activity far removed from actually understanding it. Rather, mental pictures show themselves to be like the cuckoo which surreptitiously lays its egg in the nest of another, unsuspecting bird. Not only does the cuckoo throw out and destroy one of the host bird's eggs, but the egg it leaves in its place is identical in terms of its outer appearance (though not of course beneath it). Yet the cuckoo chick also has an innate intelligence. It knows when to hatch just before its rival step–siblings, to gain a march upon them and perhaps even to destroy their eggs before they have had a chance to hatch themselves. And all the while the host bird continues to feed and nurture the alien bird until it is even bigger than itself. But never does it realize that it is really an impostor which has taken over its life. And the same is true of ourselves; like the unsuspecting host bird, we live in delusions if we cannot see beyond the surface of our thoughts as they cloak themselves in mental pictures.

★   ★   ★

Just as we can find out more about the books by opening them up, so we can reveal more about our mental pictures by opening them up too. Thus, although our mental pictures are the front line of our experience, we are also able to step beyond them. By making the activity of our thinking the intended object of our thoughts, we transform our thinking from being merely a picture of itself into an object every aspect of which is opened up to us. We might say that through this activity our mental pictures are transformed into something transparent or living. However, making our mental pictures transparent is alone not enough to tell us what they truly mean. Similarly, in terms of the bookcase, opening up a book and seeing its pages will only take us so far. We need also to understand the meaning of what is printed there.

We can leaf through each page of a book and see everything that is written or printed there; if it is a book of Braille we might instead run the tips of our fingers across the surface of each page, or if it is an activity book for children we might be better off rubbing or even smelling the pages. But simply revealing to our senses what lies upon each page is not enough. Quite different faculties are demanded of us if we are to read the different types of script we see there. We may be able to feel the raised dots of Braille, but to understand what they mean is quite another matter. If the book before us is written in Arabic script, we need an understanding of Arabic. The same is true if it is written in English, or it is a book of mathematics. Similarly, in order for us to glean information about how the book was manufactured, we need an understanding of the type of paper it is printed on, the printing process used, the choice of font, how the book has been bound together, the materials used and so on. All of this extends over and above the simple act of recognizing the book as a book.

In order to move to a more transparent level of understanding in the case of our inner life of thinking, we must endeavour to do the same. To begin with, we experience our mental pictures in relation to other mental pictures, but by doing so do not escape the fact that we may simply be comparing one appearance with another appearance or one illusion with another illusion. When we make these pictures transparent, we begin to experience one object in all its aspects (that is the activity of bringing forth a mental picture) with another object in all its aspects. However, our inner life of thinking consists of more than just mental pictures and our experience of the activity that brings these pictures into consciousness. For alongside all of this we are also beings of *feeling*, that is to say, we respond to our surroundings in an individual and unique way. What is more, we also live within a body we are able to call our own. When we are bitterly angry, desperately sad or ecstatically happy, this body undergoes a change of equilibrium. Expressed another way, each and every feeling is something which wells up within us in response to the world pressing upon us. A feeling, we might say, is a change within the equilibrium of our own being.

To begin with, we cannot be more specific than this since comprehending with any certainty what feelings actually are involves first overcoming a particular philosophical con-undrum. This arises through the dominance of mental pic-tures in our 'ordinary' thinking life such that we cannot truly say that we 'ordinarily' experience our feelings, but rather only mental pictures of them. At first this may seem con-troversial or even absurd. 'Of course we experience our feelings!' we must say. But this is exactly the problem. We do indeed experience our feelings, but *through* our thoughts, and in particular our faculty of mental picture building. What is more, the resulting picture we have of our feelings is so realistic and one to which we are so used that we are easily beguiled into believing that it is the real thing. Thus, when we are completely engulfed in emotion, it is generally the mental picture of the emotion which has overwhelmed us. When this happens, it is as if our sense of self has become drowsy or has even fallen into a dreamy sleep. But as we nod off to sleep or fall into a dream, we are not necessarily aware that we are doing so. We are immersed in pictures which are so lifelike that we are not aware that we are actually asleep. Just as a photograph or cinema image might be very realistic but must always lack in some way the vitality of the reality it represents, so the same is true of our feelings when we experience them through mental pictures. One thing supplants another, and the intended object is overlooked.

In the case of thinking, this situation can be remedied. We are able to step beyond the initial picture we have of our thoughts by making the activity of our thinking the direct content of our thoughts. We can all do this. By the same token, we might believe that our feelings can be made transparent by turning our activity of feeling into the immediate object of our thoughts. For instance, we experience the feeling of joy or sadness in relation to something. We experience this feeling as welling up within us. Indeed we can all experience this. Yet the result must be a mental picture of our feeling life. We become like a person who makes their way around a gallery looking at the reproductions in the catalogue or the postcards from the gallery shop, but inadvertently fails to look up to all the originals which are hanging on the walls right in front of them.

However, it is also reasonable to suppose that we can begin to read the book of our feeling life by making our own activity of feeling the immediate object of our feelings. This is a path we will need to explore. But in order for it to lead us anywhere it must, of necessity, require us to 'think' or 'cognize' in a radically different way, namely, with a mode of consciousness that is not dependent upon mental pictures.

★ ★ ★

We cannot say that with our faculties of mental picture building we are able to observe our feelings directly. Though we are close to them, it appears that we do not have the means to take hold of them. It is as if we have been asked to describe the underside of some great boulder, but lack the strength and the means to turn it over. It is right at our feet, but also beyond our gaze. Nevertheless, what we are able to observe when we are hungry or when we are sad is that our sense of *inner equilibrium* undergoes a change. Like the ripples (or indeed waves) which move across a lake when its equilibrium has been disturbed by something falling into it, by the wind, by rumblings from beneath its surface, so our feelings are really the ripples upon the lake of our own bodily equilibrium. Expressed another way, it is these ripples passing through us which are the basis for our feelings such that our own corporeality begins to emerge as a sense organ in its own right.[3]

We can endeavour to clarify what this means by returning our attention to the bookcase still in front of us, and to the fact that our uncovering of the secrets which lie within it takes place in a stepwise manner: seeing the bookcase; recognizing the bookcase as a bookcase; opening up of the books; reading or understanding their content and so on. As we have already seen, it is possible for us to form mental pictures of the bookcase which do not correspond with the reality before us. We might think we see a book which really is not there, or see a yellow duster but fail to recognize what it is. We 'correctly' recognize that there is an object out there but are unable to find a context for it, or place it in a false context. Similarly, when we mistakenly believe that the bookcase is made of wood when really it is not, or we mistake a row of boxes for books, we have taken the act of recognition a stage further but have still been fooled by surface characteristics. So continues the stepwise but also fluid nature of cognition. However, this also continues even after we have recognized an object 'correctly'. This becomes apparent when we consider how, when we rightly recognize a book as a book, a tree as a tree, a star as a star, or a person as a person, in each case we are still a very long way away from recognizing the full reality of what it is we have intended our thoughts towards. With any and every outer phenomenon of the world, it seems that there is always something further to uncover.

Our previous reflections upon the clock on the mantlepiece and the chairs around the table have helped to inform us how, through intending our thinking towards an object, what we have called the inherent concept is released from that object, universalized and combined with what we have called the universal concept, which at the same moment is individualized. The synthesis of these two concepts, the universalized inherent concept with the individualized universal concept is itself what we have called a mental picture. Therefore, through each cognitive step that we take, the inherent concept or concepts which permeate that aspect of the world towards which our thoughts are intended are released and thereby unified with the total existence in a universalized form from which universal concepts are individualized through our individual acts of intentionality. However, when this does not happen, when the synthesis of these two conceptual dimensions does not happen in a harmonious way, we *feel something*. The resulting mental picture does not conform with, or is a distortion of, the conceptual realities behind it. Thus, the picturing may be wrong or a half-truth, while the conceptual processes active in our

thinking are true to the intended object. It is that the formation of the mental picture has been distorted or corrupted
in some way; but *we feel this distortion as something beyond our
current mental picture.* When the act of cognition is not fully
resolved, as is particularly evident in acts of so-called mis-
perception, we feel this as a tension within us; and for each
step we take towards allowing these conceptual realities to
live undistorted within us, we feel this as a form of release.

Our striving for cognitive resolution proceeds on this basis
until we arrive at the pivotal point at which our thinking
comes face to face with the source of its own activity. In this
moment, thinking content and intended object become one.
Yet the result of such an activity can never be a mental
picture in a conventional sense, since if ever it were pictured
as such it would mean we had taken a step back to the form of
picture consciousness we are trying to overcome. Instead, we
have to do here with a *pre-picturing* or a *non-picturing*
dimension to consciousness.[4] Indeed, each and every act of
cognition has a non-picturable dimension to it. It is just that
we are not necessarily aware of it during the normal course of
our lives. (We might also arrive at this notion of non-
picturing through a process of positive exclusion in which we
endeavour to become aware of the unseeable, not only in our
faculty of mental picture building but also in a way that
extends to the transparency achievable through intending
thinking towards its own activity.)

At those moments when the level to which we are
accustomed to recognizing the world changes, we are suddenly able to feel the fluidity of our grasp upon the sense
world. It is also at such moments that we are able to feel quite
tangibly how our mental pictures do not conform with the
conceptual processes behind them. Indeed, consciousness
arises within us through the tensions between the conceptual

as it exists in the world and the conceptual as it exists in our thinking. When we engage with the world, we inevitably feel an unresolved tension deep within our own constitution. Yet as our thinking works to resolve this tension, we tangibly feel ourselves coming closer to reality. What we feel is the conceptual as it is active in our thinking flowing into the conceptual as it is released from the world. But we also *feel* this release in relation to the reference point provided by the conceptual as it permeates our own body. The rhythms in the life processes of our corporeality, which underpin our own inner life, also resonate with the rhythms and life processes of the macrocosm. As our thinking connects with the total existence in a universalized form, so our feelings, through their basis in our body's own rhythms and sense of equilibrium, resonate to a greater or lesser extent with the macrocosm in its own rhythms of waxing and waning. By bringing together the life processes as we experience them in the world with this resonance or inner movement as we experience it within ourselves, we are able to feel the veracity (or falseness) of our own individual thoughts. Then if we are able truly to feel this, it can become a feeling for the truth in the world. But as soon as we try even to think and picture this feeling we deny it its nature. We experience it as something which has reality by virtue of the fact of our own existence. It is not something which can ever be pictured, but exists purely in the tension and release in the movement of our own being and its relationship with the totality of what is around us and what has formed us.[5]

★   ★   ★

When finally we reach out a hand to take one of the volumes off its shelf we discover that it is not a book at all but an album of photographs. As we look upon one photograph after another we see how it is an album which brings together the people, the places and the events of our own life: our family, our friends, our birthdays, our holidays and the places we grew up in. While we gaze at the images collected there, the photographs also prompt us to experience a whole host of other images we do not currently see with our senses. The broad compass of this faculty to recall a mental picture of an object or event retrospectively, that is in the absence of the object itself, is generally referred to as *memory*.

Since we are wary of the fact that an image upon a photograph can become a surrogate for our original memory of the event it depicts, we close our eyes and allow our mind to wander to other events for which we know there is no photographic record: the person who took a particular photograph and is therefore not pictured upon it, the presents we received on a specific birthday alongside those who gave them to us, and so on. Such reflections go to reinforce the notion that our memories are relived from within us: the fact that we can hold on to these pictures or relive them at a later time appears to have something to do with the way we live within a body that is uniquely our own.

In order to look at this faculty of memory further, we need to summarize again how our mental pictures come into being in the first place. By intending our thinking towards the world, the sensible appearance of something withdraws as its inherent concept is released and thereby finds its connection with the rest of the world in its conceptual form. It is universalized. This takes place beyond the bounds of the human organism. But cognition is also about striving for balance. Through individualizing a concept in our thinking, a change in the physical constitution of the human being takes place as a counterbalance to the withdrawal of what is sensible in the world. For what takes place in the physical constitution which supports thinking is that it also withdraws in order that, *in its place*, a mental picture can arise within consciousness.[6] That is to say, the individualizing of a concept is marked by a withdrawal of the human organism. Consequently, in so far as the activity of thinking and consciousness is visible in the sense world, it is indirectly visible only as a momentary withdrawal of substance. Thinking and consciousness arise in the place where there is an absence of substance, such that we will outwardly 'see' this activity only if we can intend our thoughts towards something which itself cannot be pictured.

This symmetry leads to the notion that thinking activity takes place within the *negative space* which is impressed upon the human organism by individual acts of cognition. The nature of these impressions is not that they themselves are of a physical nature; rather, that they are visible (in terms of nerve-brain activity) only as the imprints upon our bodily constitution, while their active element lies beyond it and therefore beyond ordinary cognition. But these imprints are also crucial for our understanding of memory. Over time, as the experiences of our life accumulate, so these imprints also accumulate. Some of them consolidate themselves while others fade away. Nevertheless, together they form into something which holds within and about it what is really our *total existence in an individualized form*.

Our memories are special to us and therefore can be said to belong to what we may call our soul. As such, the totality of these impressions is something we are able to call our soul body. In other words, our total existence in an individualized form is also our soul body.[7] It is a dimension of our existence which is beyond our physical body. It is also that concept which defines our individual being. Therefore, just as any object in the world has an individual concept inherent to it (what we have called its inherent concept), so *we* have an individual concept inherent to us (what we have called our soul body). As far as memory is concerned, we can say, therefore, that it is possible because each and every act of cognition leaves a unique imprint upon our own inherent concept or soul body. Recollection is then an act of cognition with the same laws and principles as an act of cognition in the world, except it is truly an act of self-cognition. It involves intending our thinking activity towards a part or parts of our total existence in an individualized form or soul body. In this way a memory is relived as a mental picture within us.[8]

* * *

When we look at a photograph taken on a birthday we celebrated many years ago it causes us to reminisce upon other birthdays we have had over the years. Some birthdays we remember more clearly than others; perhaps some we cannot even remember at all. Nevertheless, memory thereby shows itself to be an act of association. Just as cognition of the world at large is about recognizing the relationships between our different sense impressions, so recollection is the same except it is an act of inner recognition within our own soul body. *Memory itself is a para-sensible body of individualized concepts which have maintained their relationship with one another.* But just as can happen in the case of acts of recognition of the outer world where we misperceive the world in the various ways already described, this can also happen for acts of recollection. The world at large is a complex play of concepts; but so is the total body of our memories. Thus, when we relive a memory, it is possible for us to miscognize this inner configuration, mixing up one memory with another. We might recall spending a birthday in such and such a place and with a particular group of people. The separate components of the memory are correct. We are right to recall spending a birthday with this particular group of people, just as we are right to recall spending a birthday in the particular place we remember. The problem is that we are confusing two different birthdays.

Memory is an act of recognition which can take place in the absence of the original phenomenon which gave rise to it because the key to the conceptual content of that phenomenon has been imprinted upon us in an individualized form. But each memory we recall requires a fresh act of recognition, of universalizing what is impressed upon us and of individualizing concepts from out of the total world existence in a universalized form. The original phenomenon can thereby be relived within us. What is more, as happens in acts of outer cognition, what we recall as a mental picture through our faculty of memory will also have a non-picturable dimension behind it. This comes about through the fact that, even though each memory we have is special to us, it will always have behind it a universal conceptual content which resonates (or otherwise) with the macrocosm as this is active in the movement and equilibrium of our own being. And since through the act of remembering, any individualized conceptual content within us may be universalized again and again, the veracity of all that we recall can, and indeed should, be tested anew each time.[9]

Another peculiarity of memory is that memories are also forgotten. Indeed, if all our life experiences were retained as memories we would not be able to function in the world. Forgetting is necessary for us; and yet something very special happens when a memory is forgotten. For the forgetting of memories is in turn the means by which we acquire faculties. But what does this mean in practice?

Walking, speaking, reading and writing, playing a musical instrument, understanding a foreign language, driving a car and playing a sport are all faculties. However, fluency in all of these requires us to forget the detailed building blocks we needed to learn in order to acquire these skills in the first place. Fluency in reading, for example, is dependent upon us forgetting how we learnt the sounds of each letter; fluency in a musical instrument requires us to forget how we learnt by rote all the fingerings, hand, arm and perhaps mouth positions necessary for the execution of individual notes; fluency in a sport requires us to forget our awkward first attempts at striking the ball and so on. A process of forgetting is vital in all of these. However, all is not forgotten; rather, it is transformed.

A memory is really a concept that has been kept in an individualized form by the soul for itself. Then when a memory is forgotten, it is in part given up by the soul and becomes universalized again. Forgotten memories are then held within a different, indeed one might say a finer, part of our soul. Together they form a more fluid conceptual body through which countless faculties are able to flow. The above are just a tiny number of these which might be sustained there. However, also dwelling alongside them is our own character. This, like our faculties, is something which is acquired and transformed over time through a process of cognizing and forgetting. Though it is not something of which we are usually fully conscious, it is intimately bound up with our existence in the world. Really it is the faculty which colours our relationship both with ourselves and the world at large.

Along with the formation of our character, this process of forgetting also has a profound bearing upon what is loosely called the subconscious. In this context, the subconscious may be understood as the vague remembrance of the otherwise forgotten memories which go to make up our total existence in an individualized form. It is those aspects of our soul which surface as memories but which have also been partially universalized into faculties. However, alongside all the forgotten experiences which have helped our development, there are also those which have hindered or disrupted it. The positive is there alongside the negative, the benign alongside the harmful. Indeed, just as there are forgotten memories which have given us positive faculties, there are also negative experiences which have been forgotten or suppressed but which have left their mark upon us as distorted faculties, leaving us sometimes profoundly disturbed or wonderfully gifted. Some of these remain in this in-between state known as the subconscious. And yet it is one of life's tasks to become aware of, and work with, all that is poisonous which may have been sown within us, as well as to realize the nourishing faculties which will also have been sown alongside it.

★　★　★

As an exercise, we make ourselves aware of an everyday object: a mug, a pen, a book, a radio and the sounds which come from it. We observe this object through our senses but are aware that we give it form through the mental picture which is created within us. We allow this picture to live within us before we then disengage our senses from the object which gave rise to it. We can do this by closing our eyes; we can also do it by touching the object and then releasing it, or in the case of the sounds from the radio, switching it off. In this way we will accustom ourselves to the notion that a mental picture applies no more to our sense of sight than it does to our other senses. That we may have a greater facility to hold onto a picture from one sensory sphere over another is something which will vary and be special to us.

We then try to experience how this mental picture is the end-product of a process. Instead of looking at the picture, time and again we turn all our attention towards the process that created it. By doing this, by observing the activity behind our thoughts, our thought pictures will begin to become transparent and qualitatively different to us. We will begin to live within them as if we are observing the world directly with our thinking. We will live amidst the feeling of like comprehending like.

However, as we do so, a feeling will always colour our engagement with the world. We experience fondness for our favourite mug, annoyance at the pen which does not write properly, excitement over the book we have to read, or anger at what we hear on the radio. But to become aware of the forming of our feelings through a faculty of soul, which is of like nature to our own feelings, we must cultivate a sense for something that cannot be pictured within us but relates instead to our experience of inner movement and inner equilibrium.

What will help us in this task is if we begin to feel directly how the balance of our whole being changes as the world impresses itself upon us and we reach out to touch it. But we should endeavour not to experience this change through our faculty of mental picture building, but as something in itself. We do so through a direct sense for the equilibrium of our own being in relation to the processes of the world. We will sense this more strongly when, after we have felt this change in relation to so-called inanimate objects, we turn our attention to things that are living. We reflect in the same way upon a cloud, a plant, an animal and finally a human being. Only then will we find the points of reference through which to cultivate a feeling for the life of the world in its relationship with the life as it pulses through us.

Chapter in a nutshell

- This chapter compares experiences of a bookcase filled with books with those of our own thoughts.

- We first become aware of a bookcase when we form a *mental picture* of it. We then find out more about the books by opening them up and reading them. However, we do not thereby overcome our individual mental pictures.

- Since forming a mental picture of something does not mean that we have recognized it correctly, feeling is examined in its capacity to penetrate behind our mental pictures and become the basis for a *feeling for truth*.

- This chapter also considers *memory* as the ability to relive a mental picture in the absence of the object that first formed it, and how the sum of our memories is impressed into what is called our *soul body*. Recollection is thereby self-observation of our own soul body.

- The process of forgetting is also characterized in relation to the development of human faculties.

12. The World as Mirror and Reflection

We receive our surroundings from our own unique perspective. These are inescapably a mixture of the natural and manufactured world. Even if we find ourselves in the most unspoilt oasis we will probably be there dressed in clothes and shoes manufactured by other people. Similarly, if we find ourselves in the most man-made of environments such as high in the air and enclosed within the cabin of an aeroplane, where even the air we breathe has been artificially produced, we might just have an apple with us as a token of our connection with the so-called natural world. At home, we might sit upon a chair made of wood while gazing across a room at a houseplant which grows within soil bounded by a plastic pot, while beyond that we look out of a window made of glass to other houses set against the skyline. So it is that we surround ourselves by objects which have the mark of other people upon them alongside the objects and processes of the natural world.

However, amidst all of these there are also those processes and objects we instigate ourselves. Our own setting in life is filled with the results of our actions, even if much of the trail we leave behind upon the earth seems to be little more than an inevitable consequence of the very fact of our existence. The turbulence and change in the composition of the air which takes place through each breath we take, or the creases, dirt and sweat we impress upon our clothes, might be as inconsequential as the footprints we leave upon melting snow. But these and everything like them are there by virtue of our individual existence, and are consequently the physical reminders of our own path through the world. They are there because of us, even if we are not always fully conscious of them as they happen. On the other hand, other actions we instigate have behind them the full weight of our faculties of consciousness. When we reach out to shake someone's hand, speak our marriage vows in front of an assembled congregation or sign our name upon our last will and testament, it is likely that we do so in a state of high wakefulness. Again in terms of their appearance alone, these are little more than a simple movement of our arm, words which as soon as they are spoken will dissipate into space, and the marks of ink upon paper. That is to say, their effects upon our physical environment are little different from scratching our leg, mumbling in our sleep or accidentally spilling a drink. Rather, their most profound difference lies in the fact that over and above their appearance to the world they have been invested by us with a particular level of *intention*.

When we look at all the many imprints we leave upon the earth in terms of everything but their appearance, what remains there as something active but unseen is an imprint of our individuality. Indeed, the level of intention we have invested into them remains impressed into the world. Expressed another way, if we look beyond their appearance, we will see there an extension of our own consciousness in a form which has become in some way external to us.

At the same time, there is also another category of object which has been invested with intentions directed specifically at us. For example, everything from a jumper knitted for us when we were a baby through to the shake of someone else's hand, like all that we set in train ourselves, would not exist were it not for us. But rather than growing out of our own thoughts and actions, they come towards us as the result of the intentional acts of others.

The world and our past will also be filled with such objects

and actions. Some will undoubtedly have been more deliberate in their creation than others, just as they are with our
own actions. Most will also probably have long since been
dissipated back into the earth from which they came, again
like much which has flowed out of our own intentions. But
somewhere in our possession, or simply in our past, there will
always be objects that we know were fashioned with us *woven
through the thoughts of their creator.*

We may possess a great number of mementos as reminders
of those individuals who brought us into the world or who
helped to nurture or educate us, or of those events we are
afraid of forgetting; or we may possess scarcely any at all. But
among the many things we may have retained, one thing that
we can be sure was created with us woven through the
thoughts of its creator is a personal letter addressed to us. Such
a letter may have come from someone we have now lost
touch with as well as from someone who has now died. It
might remind us of births and deaths, illnesses and recoveries,
the joys and misfortunes of ourselves and others, the musings
upon what life might have been as well as upon what was.
Any one letter we decided at some point in our lives to
preserve may contain world news as well as family news, or
else tell of little other than whether the day upon which it
was written was fine or rainy, hot or cold. But this apparent
ephemera still means something to us because it was written
down by someone with us in their mind.

While the creation of such objects is not arbitrary but the
result of a deliberate act on the part of another person *intended
specifically towards us,* this is not at first sight the case with the
paper the letter is written on or the ink used to write it. These
most probably will have been produced en masse by people
unaware of our existence. They appear to exist quite independently of us. We can even suppose that they would have

come into being had we died in infancy or never been born at all. But there is also a broader intentionality behind their manufacture which eventually means that they become available to us. Then once they have been fashioned together in the way we now see before us, the fact of their existence alongside one another becomes entirely dependent not only upon the writer, but also upon us.

As the physical product of a gesture on the part of another thinking being, we are interdependently connected with anything made with us in mind. It would not exist in the same way had we not also existed. It is therefore a re-action to our presence within the world. Over and above that, it also shows that the fact of our life in the world is always being reflected back upon us in one form or another through the conscious actions of others. A letter taken as a whole is a symbol for how the world is shaped out of the intentions of other beings besides ourselves. The folds of the paper and the gestures behind the flow of the ink, along with the stream of thoughts of which the words themselves are a picture, are the marks of actions intended towards us. They are the impressions of thoughts upon substance. And we can begin to *read* these marks. We find in them a connection with our-selves over and above their physical appearance. They come towards us by virtue of a consciousness which is not our own. It is as if another part of our being, or an extension of it, instead of emanating from a point within us streams towards us from the periphery of our existence.

We also live within a wider world setting. This, through *events*, comes towards us just as we reach out towards it. We are not always aware of the consciousness behind it. It is often anonymous to us. Yet there, too, we find a part of us even if it does not seem to belong to the sum total of what we our-selves have lived through hitherto. Rather, it belongs to the sum total of the intentions of the world and its beings, of which we are just one. For in seeking to understand ourselves in the context of the totality of the world, we must consider the world as it comes towards us as well as what we find within ourselves. Our existence thereby becomes a dialogue between us as conscious individuals and the summation of the consciousness of the world. By opening such a dialogue we will find that behind everything which our thoughts embrace, from what we impress upon the world ourselves, through what is created specifically for us, alongside the manufactured world in general as well as the natural world, up to and including the earth in its cosmic setting, there exists a reflection of our own being.

Chapter in a nutshell

- Our surroundings are a mixture of the natural world and objects that have been manufactured or simply bear the mark of the actions of different people.
- A fact of our existence is that we leave our own mark upon the earth. We invest every action with a different level of intention, from our unconscious breathing to our signature upon an important document. Together, these intentions form the imprint of our individuality upon the earth.
- Also active in the world are those intentions directed specifically towards us. A deliberate creation of this sort could be a letter written to us. However, this carries a different degree of intentionality to the paper and ink with which it is written.
- This chapter considers how our individual existence and intentions are woven into the intentions of all the other conscious beings of the earth.

Part V:

FREEDOM AND OUR THINKING

13. *The High Street* or *Living Within Our Own Reflection*

Simply making our way down a busy street is of itself a glittering feast for all our senses. It is also a feast which they will never be able to digest fully. Wafts of hot air flow from shop entrances on cold days, while clouds of cold emerge on hot days. The smells of freshly baked bread and patisserie are carried upon the air around bakeries and coffee shops, just as the very same air carries music of all types as it spills over onto the pavement from clothes shops and music shops. All around is the hustle and bustle of other shoppers, the drone of traffic and the general mêlée of people going about their business. Then in every direction we look are shops and more shops filled with goods and more goods.

We are free to wander in whichever direction or into whichever shop takes our fancy. With money in our pocket, a whole world of choice is opened up to us. We are at liberty to spend it exactly as we please. Yet just as we know we should not attempt to buy things we cannot afford, so we also understand that there are limits on where we can go and what we can do. For the most part we are content to abide by them, since we know full well the reasons for not stepping into the path of moving traffic or continually bumping into other pedestrians. Within the shops themselves we know that we should not go behind counters, venture into window displays or go through doors marked private. We may of course be of such an age or disposition that we find it difficult to follow rules and regulations, or simply wish to rebel against them such as through acts of shoplifting or vandalism. On the other hand, we may merely be unaware of them such as if we are in a foreign country. Nevertheless, despite these restrictions, we feel a sense of freedom in where we can go and what we can do.

With this sense of freedom running through our veins, without us even realizing it a thought is suddenly plucked from the very edge of our field of vision and before we know it we have turned our head and body to follow it. We find ourselves looking up towards a beautiful landscape. Richly coloured mountains and a sunset so red we can scarcely believe that it is real draw us out of the artificiality of our current environment and into a place that is more primal and closer to nature. Then no sooner have we entered this landscape than we are moving through it. An isolated mountain road traces its way upwards as far as our eye can see to where, close to the summit, a single speeding car shoots towards the setting sun. All of a sudden, we are behind the wheel of that car, experiencing the freedom of the road and the combined excitement of speed and power. As we look away, a few names and symbols at the base of the mountains catch our attention. Then as quickly as the experience came into our consciousness, so it vanishes into nothing. We are not even sure whether it leaves a mark upon us since the deserted mountain road in all its beauty is soon forgotten in favour of fresh impressions and fresh experiences.

In one direction we see images intended to flatter, while in another we see images which instil in us fear. Loud music meant to make us feel good about ourselves comes from one shop, while a headline in front of a newspaper vendor tells us of the latest disaster to hit the world. Our head turns in the direction of where the music is coming from and we see a pristine shop window filled with immaculately dressed mannequins. No sooner have we done so than we find ourselves imagining how we might feel if we were dressed like one of them in all the latest and most fashionable clothes. Indeed, the picture we create of ourselves is so strong that it causes us momentarily to take on the appearance of these inanimate objects. We project ourselves into their place. Then, without us even asking, this plays upon all our vulnerabilities regarding our appearance, our sexuality and our general standing in society. Quite involuntarily we end up asking ourselves: how do we really look to the eyes of the outside world?

As we turn once more in order to continue on our way, new impressions supersede the old. What just a few seconds ago was so real and immediate to us is again forgotten. A travel agent window tempts us with possibilities of escape to far-away places. A little farther on, we feel pleased with ourselves because we see something in a shop window with a price tag higher than what we have just paid for the very same article in another shop. However, in the chemist window next door, warnings of the dangers of high blood pressure and heart disease direct our thoughts to the fact of our own mortality. This soon expands into a whirlwind of worry as to whether we are likely to die of cancer, a heart attack or a stroke, or whether our mind and memories will fade away until we no longer know who we are.

In the same chemist's window, pictures of bespectacled eyes, greying hair and white teeth conjure up within us a whole host of images of ourselves and how we might look to others. Then before we know it we are sidestepping a few paces back and forth to where the window darkens just enough for us to make out our own reflection beyond it. We see there our eyes blinking, the hair on our head and, just when we smile to ourselves, our front teeth framed by our lips. We see all these things, yet we also know that, like the images we had of ourselves before we looked at our reflection, our experience is again of pictures we create for ourselves. We know that if we insist on *seeing* our eyes, our teeth and the hair on the back of our head, we must for ever content ourselves with pictures, since these are just those parts of our body which we can never see with our own eyes directly. Then just as our thoughts and the pictures which go with them continually stand between us and the whole of the created world, so it can also seem that our experience of this, too, is no more than a reflection of something we will never see directly.

★   ★   ★

So it is that the more our inner life conforms to the outer appearance of the world, the more we come to believe that our thoughts are a reflection of a world external to them. Like a picture, our thoughts become two-dimensional, where any sense of depth or space is just an illusion. Furthermore, since images of the external world are the most visible part of our thoughts they come to dominate our thinking as a whole. In fact, for all intents and purposes, they become our thoughts. Indeed, the surface veneer of our thinking is so dominated by images created by outer impressions that at times we have to look deep within us to find those thoughts we are really able to call our own.

Often, if we are not vigilant, by living ever more amongst the outer images we have of the world, we will not notice that our thinking becomes increasingly a passive 'activity'. Our thoughts simply follow our perceptions, while the thoughts we do have independently of current perceptions seem to mirror previous perceptions. In this way, the sense world comes to fill the entire horizon of our attention such that our thoughts scarcely have an independent existence of their own.

This is further accentuated by the way one impression follows another. This results in the appearance that our sensations lead our thoughts, and not our thoughts our sensations. Indeed, our thoughts seem to dance to and fro on the end of invisible marionette strings, while the pace of this dance is defined by a puppeteer who is not ourselves but our environment. This in turn makes it still more difficult for us to believe that thinking can have a life of its own since our own processes of thought are continually coerced into becoming ever more like the processes of the external world. We do not think to stretch out our arms in order to try and experience with our sense of touch the space beyond the tips of our fingers since to do so requires us to become aware of something which we cannot directly perceive. Instead, our thoughts become derivative of our environment until finally it seems that we no longer *think* but *are thought*.

Chapter in a nutshell

- A busy shopping street is a feast for our senses.
- At the same time, the sensations that surround us are so powerful that they are able to pull thoughts and emotions out of us without us really having control over them. Some are so strong that we even lose ourselves within them.
- We come across our reflection in a shop window. What we see there is no more than a picture; it is not us as we truly are.
- As pictures of the world dominate our thinking, we come to believe that it is our sensations which lead our thoughts and not our thoughts which give our sensations form.
- This chapter considers some of the difficulties associated with freeing ourselves from the notion that thinking forms only pictures of a world external to it.

14. Words, Freedom and Our Search for Meaning

On the table in front of us sits an old-fashioned dictionary made of paper, card, webbing for the spine, glue and of course ink. Together, the ink and paper form shapes which we have learnt to decipher as words. We then attach meaning to these words so that within the dictionary they can be used to describe other words. Just as individual words have specific meanings, so the received meaning of the relationship between words is something we understand as language. Together they form links in a long alphabetical chain of words and their definitions or their equivalents in other languages, depending on what sort of dictionary it is.

As well as having a definition of the word 'definition', a dictionary is such that it must also contain a definition or translation of itself. Indeed, the recurring consequence of the self-referential nature of a dictionary is that the words used for the definition of 'dictionary', such as 'book', 'alphabetical', 'word', 'language' and 'meaning' must also have their own entry in other parts of the dictionary where new words or the same words in new contexts are used to describe them. Thus, the definition of the word 'meaning' uses such words as 'what', 'means' and 'concept'. The word 'concept' then uses such words as 'idea', 'notion' and 'abstract'. And so it goes on until the whole book forms a corpus of knowledge which has meaning not only for us but also for other people.

However, the dictionary might be printed in a language we cannot read a single word of. We are therefore unable to fulfil its intended meaning as something to be read, assimilated and understood (or at least not without a tremendous amount of deciphering work) since we no longer relate to the shapes upon the pages *as words*. Instead, because of its size and weight we may have decided at some point in the past that this object which for others is a dictionary for us makes an ideal flower press (as well as an occasional doorstop). That is why it is on the table in front of us (because we wish to press flowers), and not because we wish to look up the meaning of different words. Though the way we think about the dictionary and our subsequent actions in relation to it are totally alien to its original function, it nevertheless has *meaning for us*. Its meaning in the world (as our favoured tool for pressing flowers) has been determined by the individual way in which *we* think and relate to it. Furthermore, as well as having a practical function, we also gain a certain aesthetic pleasure from its general appearance, from the feel of its pages between our fingers, its dusty old smell and sight of its diverse printed forms and colours. It is thus also a decorative object we enjoy having around; but as a dictionary, it means nothing to us.

Just as these vagaries and variations in meaning apply to dictionaries and their usage, so they also affect the words themselves, albeit in slightly different and more subtle ways. Even if we do understand fully the language the dictionary is written in, and we are using it exactly in the way it was intended, it is no less dependent upon us and the way we think about it for its meaning than if we are using it as a flower press or doorstop. However clear and precise the definitions contained in it are, the words that go to make up any one definition are still subject to the individual way in which we relate to them. We must admit that they are also prone to our own unique whims, fancies and associations.

In practice, the meaning of any word is dependent upon a

whole plethora of mental pictures which come to us by means of memory and association. These, and the nature of their relationships with one another, are dependent upon the sum of our individual experiences throughout our life up to and including the present moment. Any one word will therefore inevitably mean constantly varying things to different people; or expressed another way, our relation to any one word is unique as well as continually evolving within ourselves. For example, the mental picture or pictures called forth by the word 'tree' (or its equivalent in other languages) will always fluctuate depending on our experience of trees throughout our lifetime hitherto. If we have spent all our life in a desert area we will form very different mental pictures based on the word tree than if we have spent our life in an area dominated by coniferous forest or deciduous forest. Our relationship with the word 'elephant' will differ greatly depending on whether we have actually seen one in the flesh, whether the animal we saw was African or Asian, whether we saw it in the wild or semi-wild, in a zoo or just in a picture-book, or indeed not at all. The way we relate to the words 'aeroplane' or 'spaceship' will revolve around whether we have touched one, been in one, flown in one, seen one close up and so on. The same is true of our whole spectrum of senses. Thus, our relationship with the words 'pineapple' or 'tuna' will not just vary pictorially depending upon whether we have seen a pineapple plant growing from the ground or a tuna fish swimming in the sea, but also in terms of touch, smell and taste depending upon whether we have eaten either of them fresh or only out of a tin.

The sum of our life experiences have a bearing upon our relationship to any one word and its meaning, as well as to how words are used together, and everyone's life experiences are different. In the case of words which describe objects which are there for all to see and touch, some form of consensus can usually be reached. In the case of the words 'constellation', 'spirit' or 'soul', which refer to things that are not immediately apparent to our senses, agreement is more elusive simply because we cannot fall back upon what we see and touch. This is reinforced by the widely differing meanings and significance attributed to these words both within and across cultures, varying to an extent that some would deny them any meaning at all, considering them to be little more than empty words, while others may consider them to denote concepts central to their very existence. Something similar is also the case when we come to consider words such as 'beauty' or 'ugliness'. Across peoples and cultures, one person's beauty is often another person's ugliness, and vice versa. However, we should also be wary of believing that just because we have given something a name we know what it is. It is easy to talk about light and darkness, sweet and sour, hot and cold, or indeed just apples and oranges, but without really entering into the essence of what it is we have given a name to. Complacency can all too easily lure us into using words to describe other words, without us ever really becoming aware of the realities that stand behind them.

When we leaf through our dictionary and come across the word 'freedom', the difficulties associated with its meaning appear no less severe. Its definition is again just a sequence of words whose meanings are defined in other parts of the dictionary and to which we, as individuals, should expect to have our own personal relationship. We find there such words as 'right', 'think', 'choose', 'act', 'hindrance' and 'without', and thereby come face to face with the problem that our relationship with these words will differ just as it does for other people. We will also bring them into relationship with one another in different ways, that is, we will interpret them differently. Expressed another way, the mental pictures we form of these words, as well as the mental pictures we have of the relationships between them, will always mean different things to different people. Nevertheless, as we know in the case of trees, elephants, aeroplanes and spaceships, and even such notions as constellations, soul and spirit, we are still able to communicate and converse with other people on many subjects even if the mental pictures we have of them are different. Thus, we are able to communicate on the subject of freedom, even if we do not at first share a common notion as to what it is.

★   ★   ★

A word and the mental picture it calls forth can be a point of departure; but it will always have its limitations. This is undoubtedly the case with possible definitions for the word 'freedom'. As a point of departure a definition of freedom might, for example, consider a person's right or ability to think, speak or act as they choose without restraint or hindrance. It might also speak of the expression or fulfilment of free will. It can say all of these things, yet on the face of it, in terms of their paper-and-ink existence within the dictionary or other document, such definitions have the tendency to lay down a paper trail which may well lead us back to the conclusion that definitions themselves are no more than words about words. Similarly, when we come to transfer statements about freedom to practical situations, the same self-referential problems do not go away.[1] For example, in the general case, when faced with an identical situation and identical choices, individuals will relate to them differently because no two people's life-experiences are the same. The mental pictures they bring will never be the same as other people's. Therefore, any notion of freedom based upon mental pictures, and in particular one based on freedom of choice between mental pictures, will always lack universality. What is more, as soon as the notion of freedom is itself formed into a mental picture, as soon as it is fixed in our thoughts as an individualized idea, as soon as it is defined in words, it must lose its universality and become at best relative and at worst just an illusion. On the other hand, if a universal notion of freedom is our goal, it must exist in a form that is universal to all people. It must in some way be beyond the content of thinking and free of our mental pictures and their determining influence.

To live in mental pictures is to exist in a condition that is vulnerable to illusion and deception. We can even go so far as to say that, when we think in mental pictures, we do not have freedom in terms of the content of our own thoughts. However, when faced with an identical situation and identical choices, *what any number of individuals will have in common as they confront the world is that they are conscious thinking beings.*

At the root of every action we undertake, and preceding every choice we make, there must always be a more or less conscious process of thinking. We cannot escape the fact that behind every word we speak, behind every action we undertake, behind every choice we make, there must always be some sort of enabling thought. When we speak without thinking, act without thinking or even make a choice without really thinking, a thought is there directing us, but it is below the level of consciousness we might wish or expect of ourselves. To begin with, this process of thinking appears to be an individual one based upon the nuances in the configuration of our senses and the summation of our life experiences. It seems that our individual mental pictures and their surrogates, words, are the very warp and weft of our consciousness. Yet by looking behind the tapestry they create, we begin to become aware of the gestures that wove them into being. When we turn our attention towards anything at all and so form a mental picture of it, we individualize a universal concept from out of the total world existence in a universalized form. At the same moment, we universalize an inherent concept from out of the conceptual structure behind the perceptible world. This process of *conceptual synthesis* is a precondition for cognition and recognition to happen in the first place. It is universal. We are a vessel for this meeting of concepts out of which an individualized picture is formed. But prior to this process of individualization, what lives conceptually within us is the same for all people. These living concepts are also beyond our physical body. Indeed, our physicality withdraws so that this conceptual union can take place.

Words have meaning by virtue of our being conscious of them. However, when we think in words and mental pictures, at any one moment, our individual pictures, meanings and associations are living alongside the universal concepts and relationships from which they have been individualized. A word is a picture beyond which something universal is living. Thus, although any mental picture we have of any one aspect of the world is special and unique to us, its conceptual wellspring is beyond our own individual view of the world. The conceptual or *spiritual* wellspring of all world knowledge, and therefore all language, is the same for *all* people. It is the individualized pictures (and words) we have of the world within our *soul* and the individual ways in which those pictures have been configured and transformed by us over time and throughout our lives that are different.

Thus, although we are compelled to remain within the element of thinking, thinking also provides us with an opening whereby our thoughts can expand into something truly all-encompassing. Indeed, our thinking has the potential to experience the world in a way which is not conditioned by the words or mental pictures we have formed in our life hitherto, but as if the world would speak to us directly *in a language beyond words*. And if we enable phenomena to reveal themselves to our thinking directly we can, as individuals, open up the way towards seeing beyond the beguiling pictures of the so-called outside world and thereby to a *transformative notion of freedom*.

★   ★   ★

Our thinking is the magic spyglass through which each of us is compelled to understand both ourselves and our place in the world. However, with this compulsion also comes a gift. Though we cannot escape our thinking or look into the world without it, we have the freedom to direct it in all manner of directions, including towards its own emergence. That we do not generally do so means that any awareness of the processes by which our mental pictures are formed is constantly being squeezed out of us. We revel instead in the superabundance of perceptions which in turn seem to satisfy our thoughts. We can of course attempt to shut ourselves off from our environment, but this will no more liberate us than the flood of sensory impressions which are so much a part of life. However, the fact that we can intend our thinking in many directions and with ever more refined degrees of focus means that we are not compelled always to live a life in pictures. For as soon as we intend the magic spyglass of our thinking towards the manner of formation of our mental pictures, that is towards our own activity of thinking, our whole relationship with the world suddenly changes.

Thus, not only are we able to direct our attention towards the dictionary and then the vase containing some cut flowers which happens to be standing beside it, but also to the fact that we are doing so. Through an intentional act of thinking, a mental picture of the vase and its flowers is conjured up within us. However, to us it is not just a picture. It is a picture which has a relationship to us and to which we are able to assign certain attributes. We recognize the vase as a vase and the flowers as flowers and know that they are standing in a thing called water. We recognize the flowers' colours and can assign those colours names. Perhaps we even have a name for the flowers. It is likely that we also have words at our disposal, such as rounded, tapered or rectangular, which we can use to describe the shape of the vase. We also have a picture of our own self in relation to the flowers. We have a picture of whether we like them or dislike them. Furthermore, the fact that the vase was placed upon the table by us also means that we recognize the imprint of our actions upon its location and its relationship with the other objects on the table. We also recognize something of ourselves in the way the flowers have been cut to size and arranged within the vase. We have an individual relationship with the flowers through our actions upon them and our feelings in response to them.

On this basis, therefore, we can describe our relationship with the world in general as a *trialogue* between our living within the concepts of the world, our responding to them in terms of our feelings, and the impressions of our thoughts via our actions upon the world. In terms of the flowers and our relationships to them, these may be summarized as, firstly, our living within the concepts of the flowers; secondly, our feelings for them; and thirdly, the results of our actions upon them. Expressed another way, we think about the flowers, we have feelings for the flowers, and we imprint our *will* upon them. However, of its own accord, this trialogue does not enter our consciousness. To do so it needs our active participation, otherwise we will experience it only as a three-way conversation between a series of pictures. It will never become truly real to us.

★   ★   ★

Our own personal connections to the flowers may extend in all manner of directions. We may, for instance, have grown them ourselves. On the other hand, they may have been presented to us as a romantic gesture by someone we know, or we may simply have bought them from a shop from someone we do not know. Then if they were bought from a shop they will have arrived there by means of a whole economic, transportation and manufacturing process which, through its many and diverse relationships, must extend in ever wider and wider circles. The same is true of the vase. The person or people who fashioned it are unknown to us, as are all those who prepared the raw materials for their use and supplied the energy and transport necessary for the vase's production. The origin of the water and those concerned with collecting and delivering it to us are also unknown to us. Nevertheless, this all stands behind the flowers and vase as a factual reality. It is the total picture of how the vase, flowers and water came to be in front of us. It is, in a physical sense, their process of becoming which is visible through ordinary acts of cognition.

Simply recognizing something or giving it a name does not mean that we have recognized the being or essence behind it. What we do know is that without the activity of thinking our perceptions (that is to say our raw experience), in so far as they are the means by which our senses mediate impressions of our environment to us, must always remain barren. They need the germinating power of our thinking in order that life is breathed into them. This is what enables us to experience the world through individual pictures in the first place. However, we will not live within the activity of our thinking or even be aware of its existence unless we intend our thinking towards it. Therefore, by not only turning our attention to the vase and flowers, but also to the fact that we are doing so, we immediately bring to life the double sided nature of thinking: that it can direct itself to its own process of becoming as well as to the world. We also thereby carry out the most primal *free act* we, as human beings, are capable of.

Through this free act the vase and flowers are transformed from a picture into something living within us. Indeed, by thinking *the relationship between the world as appearance and the emergence of that appearance within us* we experience the phenomena of the world as they stream though our activity of thinking before they are changed by us into a semblance of themselves. We create a space within our thinking in which the vase and flowers are supported as living beings within us. Doing so is the first step we are able to take towards freeing ourselves from the mental pictures which otherwise dominate our consciousness. For if we really live in the process of conceptual synthesis which takes place during cognition, the relationships between and beyond what our senses perceive will become as real and immediate to us as what we otherwise perceived with our senses alone. When we transform our thinking in this way, we will truly be using our *thinking as a sense organ in its own right*.

That being so, we are not in any way bound by this since we also have the potential to reflect upon *this process of reflection*. By thinking the flowers in terms of their *relationship with the relationships which fashioned them* we move to a quite different order of cognition again. We can go some way towards realizing this when we begin to experience the relationships inherent in the flowers and vase, but in relation to the conceptual beings behind the totality of all that has formed them. The flowers would not have grown without the sun and the earth, the flow of water and the constellations of insects and other life which live in the darkness and the light, in the soil and the air, in the warmth and the cold. As all of these have relationships inherent to their own being, so all of these relationships also exist in relation to those in the vase and flowers. By *feeling* this next order of relationships, we are in fact intending our thinking towards something that is already one step removed from our mental pictures of the world and of ourselves. It is a mode of cognition that exists entirely within a dimension of non-picturing. That we are able to become aware of such a thing in the first place is enabled by the way in which we experience this non-pictured element of our thinking in relation to the inner movement which is a precondition for the fact of our own being, that is through a transformation of our feeling life. It is this which provides our point of reference, just as we can only experience darkness in relation to light, and light in relation to darkness.

There is, however, one further act of reflection we are able to undertake. This dimension of thinking mirrors the most primal quality of the sense world: the fact of its own coming into being. The clay, the glaze, the substance of the flowers as well as the water they stand in—each was all brought into existence at some point through a primal act of *intentional will*. It must have had an absolute beginning without which the present encounter would not be possible. We do not see any of this. However, the substance of the flowers bears within it the imprints of will relating to the very fact of its existence. These are an echo of the substance's *becoming*, as well as a pre-echo of what must happen *after this becoming*. They are a mirror of the totality of existence.

We can go a little way towards realizing this when we reflect upon our non-pictured experience of the flowers and vase no longer in relation to the fact of our own existence, but now in relation to the world totality. We might say that our non-picturing experience is something like a footprint in the earth; it has form but with an absence of substance. When we reflect upon this footprint further we give it life and it becomes positive again, and we return to something akin to our initial act of reflection (that achieved by using our thinking as a sense organ in its own right), but now in its total relationship with everything else. Thus, by this means, we return to the particular form and gesture of the phenomenon before us, but in its cosmic setting. And since we ourselves are a part of this world totality, it is only in this mode of cognition that we can truly say that we become *one with what we are observing*.

It is by recognizing these impressions of intentional will upon the world that human cognition attains its full resolution. It is through this focus of reflection that we can penetrate fully and transparently into all the strata of the world by means of active and awake thinking. These strata, be they of a spiritual, soul or physical nature exist in all directions, in all space and all time. They are omnipresent. When we live in the quality and gestures of this mode of thinking, we live in the gestures that originally fashioned the earth. We can have a feeling for this in relation to the processes of becoming within and beyond the substance of our own body. But we will only do so through a state of pure thinking which itself takes place beyond our physical body. Yet by this means, there cease to be any limits to revealing what lies beyond the sense world. By turning our attention towards the compass of relationships as they weave through our cosmos of thought, our experience of the world is able to expand in ever wider circles.

★   ★   ★

We are free to muse upon all of these things, even if their attainment appears at first far removed from our present relationship with the world. Nevertheless, the path that leads towards freedom in cognition begins from what we know, and not from what we don't know. It leads from any object, any encounter, any situation, and is possible at any moment of our waking existence. The sensory bombardment characteristic of modern life presents its own special challenges. It creates a veil of particular complexity and is of such a density that it has a tendency to siphon off much of our power of attention. Yet however it presents itself to us, the sense world is always in a process of becoming; and the notion of becoming is also deeply connected with an object's soul-spiritual foundation, of which the physical object is the end result. Beyond the flowers, the water they stand in and the vase which supports them, there are always other layers of reality which extend beyond the directly sense-perceivable. We find these worlds within ourselves. We see them in our own physicality, in our own processes of growth and decay which underpin our life in the world, in our sense of awareness as thinking beings, and finally through our I as beings of self-awareness. All of these provide reference points for our cognition of the rest of existence so long as we are able to experience them within ourselves not as semblance or pictures, but as realities.

Finally, words and language are also pictures beyond which a cosmos of relationships is active. Though they are tools intimately connected with our thoughts and are often our principal means for communicating with others, if we do not experience fully what is active behind them we cannot truly say that our use of them is in any way free. Words, by their nature, are also the end result of a process of becoming which is deeply connected with their soul and spiritual foundation. In so far as we are able to intend our thinking towards the manner in which words are brought to our consciousness, whether from within or without, we have the possibility to experience them as pure non-pictorial gestures. And it is by this means that we are potentially free in our faculty of language, as well as in our thinking generally. Just as the potential exists for us to make the whole process of cognition transparent, so this same potential exists for us to make transparent the intention behind words.

When we leave behind us the words and pictures which are woven through our thoughts, and step outside the self-referential constraints which go with them, we allow our thinking to live freely as a self-sustaining and self-validating activity in its own right. By doing so, our thinking, and in turn our words, will become ever more transparent to us. Freedom, as concept and activity, is thereby no longer a word, but a realization of our potential for complete transparency in our thinking, and therefore complete transparency in our relationship with ourselves and the world. Freedom can only be achieved through transparency in thinking, while the striving for transparency in thinking is an entirely free act.

★　　★　　★

As an exercise, we consider our relationship with an object—a match we have just used to light a candle, the candle or the flame itself, a tree which stands before us, the clock which tells us the time or the chair we sit on and which supports us. To begin with we make ourselves aware of the picture nature of our experience, that through our pictures we are at first detached from the world. We then bring to awareness the fact that since we have recognized the object we must also have entered into an individual relationship with it. This relationship exists quite independently of whether we are touching the object or not, since it enters us not through our senses but through our thoughts.

From here we change the focus of our attention from the content of our thoughts to the activity behind them. We will thereby begin to live within the conceptual weaving of our thinking which takes place prior to the forming of individual thoughts. We experience this directly in relation to ourselves as beings who are also emerging as well as continually passing over into a different state, and indeed our own physicality steps aside in order that the conceptual being of an object can live within us. In all that we encounter, we are able to live within an object's quality of transition, as we ourselves live in a continual state of moving from one condition to another.

We can imagine that this state of consciousness is like approaching a window through which there is a familiar view. We come nearer and discover that it is just a picture. However, by means of our own power of thinking, we can make this picture transparent and so look through to what is beyond it.

In this condition of 'beyondness' we come to something we cannot picture at all, but which we nonetheless know to be real. We are encountering the object again: our match, our candle, our chair. But it is now an experience entirely free of sense content and filled in its place with a non-picturable content which we know to be there because it resonates with the inner movement and equilibrium of our own being. We might say that it is an encounter with our original object which we now experience as consisting of everything except what we would normally picture by means of sense experience. For what we seek to experience is not nothingness, but something which is fully imbued with relationship in and about itself as well as having relationship to the fact of our own existence.

Chapter in a nutshell

- A dictionary provides us with a template for our experience of language and meaning generally.
- While recognizing the common meanings of words, we

also bring meanings and pictures that are unique to us. This applies to the word freedom as to any other. So long as our understanding is based upon mental pictures, our notion of freedom will always differ from that of every other person and therefore be a limited one.

- We direct our thinking towards a vase filled with cut flowers. While doing so, we make ourselves aware of our thinking's own emergence, thereby creating a space where the living being of the object before us can begin to reveal itself.
- We do this in three stages. Firstly, we live in the pure concepts of the world. Secondly, we bring these into relation with our feelings and sense of inner movement as corporeal beings tuned to the totality of existence. Thirdly, we open ourselves to the gesture behind the very fact of the earth's existence, of which we are part.
- This leads to transparency in all aspects of our thinking, including our use of language.
- This chapter presents the idea that striving towards transparency in thinking leads to freedom in thinking, which is itself the most primal free act we are capable of.

15. The Pencil and Us

In our hand we hold a lead pencil which we have been using to write down our thoughts. When we are finished, rather than putting it down, we take some time to look at what is written upon the pencil's hexagonal shaft. There, stamped in gold-coloured relief, is the name of the manufacturer, the place and country where it was made, and two consecutive letters in bold capitals: HB. We roll it back and forth between our fingers, feeling its glossy paint and then its sharpened point before slipping it away, blunt end first, into a pocket. From that moment on it moves with us into the future, just as what it leaves behind are the marks of our past actions: thoughts transformed into scribbles traced upon now scattered sheets of paper.

As we move through the world, so does the pencil. Sometimes we are conscious of its existence at our side, while at other times events overtake us and we are not. At these moments it could fall from our pocket and we would not know that it had gone. However, periodically we feel for its shape beneath our clothes and each time are reassured that it is still there. It moves with us as we step onto a train and journey through open countryside. It stays with us as we enter a town and then leave the train in order to travel further by bus. All the while, different people come and go; no two people are making the same journey as us. We stay on the bus until finally it swings round in a circle as it reaches its terminus where everybody except the driver gets off. From there we travel on foot, our eyes scanning the street for signs directing us to where we wish to go. In our searchings, along the pavement in front of us we see a man coming towards us with a long white cane held out before him, testing his way. As we come nearer, we see that his eyes are covered by dark glasses. We think to ask him for directions when all of a sudden the need disappears. It is not our eyes which inform us that we are virtually at our journey's end, but our sense of smell. It is this sense which suddenly helps to conjure up in us memories of schooldays passed with grubby hands gained from sharpening pencils while collecting the shavings in the palm of our hand. We cannot help recalling how, as these shavings are created, they are always accompanied by a smell that is quite unlike any other. Now, as we stand on a street corner, that very same smell is in the air.

We walk in the direction of where we believe the smell to be coming from before finally seeing the sign which confirms what we already know to be the case: that we have arrived at *the pencil factory*. This is just a temporary point of arrival for our physical body, our physical senses and the physical course of our life. For the pencil, however, it is a journey back to the place where it was once not whole, but simply parts. It is a return to the place upon the earth where all the many different ingredients necessary for its manufacture were brought together. However, these parts which make up the physical form of the pencil did not begin their existence in this place. Their different journeys reach right across the globe and far back in time to the earth's distant past.

★   ★   ★

The black lead used for the core of our pencil was once living wood which was then engulfed by molten rock before being deprived of air and left to turn slowly from vegetable to mineral. Then after spans of time it was brought to this one place from parts of the earth which now have names such as Sri Lanka, Korea and China before being ground and mixed together with clay whose origins are equally ancient. Finally this mixture was moulded and extruded into the long thin shape that is familiar to us as a pencil lead and then fired with heat in order to give it the perfect balance of hardness and blackness suited to a tool for writing. Then the wood which holds this lead, though less ancient, was still older in its forming than our own life spent upon the earth up to now. It came from a giant cedar tree which, even though it took root before pencils were invented, was destined because of the straightness of its grain for this singular human purpose. Its wood, imbued with the incense that is so familiar to us, experienced during the period of its growth the passing of centuries and the transformation of its surroundings. Then from its state of living oneness within a forest on the western edge of North America it was felled and gradually cut into smaller and smaller pieces until finally it found itself as part of no more than a humble wooden slat about to be dried and waxed before being packed off around the world. Only in this place where we are now was it joined together with another slat of wood and bonded around its core of hardened black lead before finally being cut into the six-sided shape which nestles so comfortably between our fingers.

Though a pencil now, this was not yet the object we carry in our pocket. This plain wooden form needed to be painted, dried and stamped with the name of its manufacturer in order that it could lead us back to this place of its origin. Then last but not least it had to be sharpened to a fine point, packaged and dispatched around the country to where we were able to buy it for ourselves.

This is what happened in the past. It is the outline of the story of how our pencil came to be. However, as we stand at the factory gates we know that none of this would have been possible without the role played by human intentionality and human ingenuity. Without these acting upon the substances of the earth, our pencil would never have come into being. This place, therefore, is also a focal point for a whole spectrum of acts of human intention, all of them playing their part in the transformation of substance and the final creation of this object which we now consider to be our own possession. In this sense the pencil, as well as being a physical object we are able to hold between our fingers, is also a point of in-streaming for human consciousness and human will working together with forces and events active right from the earth's ancient past. In its purest form, it is a condensing into a single object of human intentionality as it acts upon the earth's own forces of growth and transformation.

The world thereby streams into this little object in our pocket. However, when we come to consider it with our thoughts, we experience not an in-streaming but an out-streaming. Indeed, our thoughts seem to flow against the tide of the sense world. As the pencil is the result of an in-streaming whose origins are limitless, so our thoughts about it are characterized by an out-streaming which knows no boundaries. For although they begin with the specific pencil, it is from there that our thoughts are able to breathe out in all directions.

Whereas the creation of the pencil was a densification of intentionality into substance, our thoughts about it are a sublimation of all that has ever borne a relationship to it and an unfolding towards ever greater transparency. For just as the final stage in the pencil's production was the sharpening of its point, so the ultimate stage in our thinking about it is a thought-embrace that encompasses the *total reality of all that has ever come into relationship with it*. This knows no limits and, in its turn, becomes an expression of the inexpressible within and about an object from our everyday life.

Chapter in a nutshell

- We hold a pencil which we have been using to write down our thoughts.

- We then take this pencil on a journey back to the place of its manufacture where each of its elements was brought together to form a whole. These came from all over the world, while their primal origin reaches back to the earth's distant past.

- However, this pencil would not have come into being without human intentionality acting upon the earth's substance. The pencil is therefore a point of *in-streaming* for human consciousness and a condensing into a single object of human intentionality.

- Conversely, our thinking about it is characterized by the quality of *out-streaming*.

- This chapter considers how thinking expands outwards beyond the sense world and ultimately knows no limits.

AFTERWORD AND
ACKNOWLEDGEMENTS

We live in an age where information and facts dominate our thinking. This book, by contrast, ostensibly contains no information or facts. My approach to philosophy has nevertheless been a practical one, achieved principally through considering how thinking makes sense of everyday objects and situations, from the night sky through to a busy shopping street. More specifically, I have endeavoured to place the activity of thinking itself under scrutiny. In doing so, my intention has been to give philosophy something of a transformational quality, revealing possible ways of thinking which are latent within any individual, but which have not yet—for whatever reason—been uncovered. Another characteristic of this book is that I have not gone down the path of argument and counter-argument. This is not to say that what I have written should not be questioned. Rather, it is my belief that if something truly lives within someone's experience it becomes by default the one thing they are best able to question. That is why I have attempted only to present situations and ideas that can be tested by anyone as part of their everyday life, so long as they have the wish to do so.

Yet for all its intended immediacy, a profound debt to the past runs through this book. At the end of the nineteenth century and the beginning of the twentieth, the philosopher Rudolf Steiner (1861–1925) was considering the nature of human thinking in new and radical ways. He believed that the faculty of thinking is not displaced from the world, but intimately connected with it. Through his own philosophical works he attempted to set out the notion that, as self-aware beings, we are capable of attaining unprejudiced knowledge, but only when we enable our thinking to live freely within us. This, he expounded, will lead us from individual knowledge to universal knowledge. I also owe a debt, though to a lesser extent, to the philosopher Edmund Husserl (1859–1938) whose study of the consciousness of time was part of the inspiration for the central chapter of this book. Finally, I would like to acknowledge the philosophical work of Herbert Witzenmann (1905–88), whose rigorous reworking of Rudolf Steiner's original concepts has also been a source of much help and encouragement.

Anyone attempting to write a book based on the ideas of the great thinkers from the past faces many obstacles. Foremost among these is the feeling that it is probably impossible to improve upon how those ideas were presented in the first place. This is certainly the case here. That is why I have endeavoured to write a book *out of* these philosophies, and not simply a book *about* them. The feeling which grows out of a study of Rudolf Steiner's philosophical works in particular is that they are more about *activity* than *content*, more about *discovering* than they are about *learning*. They are like a transforming mirror that is able to reflect universal human faculties as well as individual human potentialities. The special nature of this legacy, however, means that any work written today which is indebted to Steiner's philosophy will best represent its universal quality when, as well as being faithful to it, it also strives to be true to itself.

We might ask what it means for something to be true to itself. Valid answers to valid questions are those which are able to live in the thoughts of an individual in such a way that they can then test them against their own experience of the world. Only in that way does *knowledge* become *living knowledge.* That we are all thinking beings capable of self-reflection means that we can ask questions of ourselves and the world. This book, in its way, is a personal meander through some of the many possibilities that are open to such a questioning attitude of mind. The fruits of that questioning, hopefully, will be both true to themselves and a contribution towards transforming philosophy into a living, breathing process.

The writing of a book can never be a solitary process. I therefore acknowledge with gratitude all the help and support I have received throughout its creation. This ranges from help with proofreading, editing and practical suggestions of various sorts, through many words of encouragement, to chance encounters with people who perhaps without their even knowing it have contributed in some way towards this book being what it is. Finally, the production of a book is also dependent upon financial and material support, and in that regard I gratefully acknowledge assistance from the Living Art and Science Trust.

Richard Bunzl,
Hebden Bridge, 2007

BIBLIOGRAPHY

Husserl, Edmund

The Idea of Phenomenology [*Die Idee der Phänomenologie* (1907)], translated by William Alston and George Nakhnikian, Kluwer Academic Publishers, Dordrecht, Boston, London 1995
On the Phenomenology of the Consciousness of Internal Time (1893–1917) [*Zur Phänomenologie des inneren Zeitbewusstseins (1893–1917)*], translated by John Barnett Brough, Kluwer Academic Publishers, Dordrecht, Boston, London 1991

Steiner, Rudolf

A Theory of Knowledge Implicit in Goethe's World Conception [*Grundlinien einer Erkenntnistheorie der Goetheschen Weltanschauung*, Berlin and Stuttgart 1886], translated by Olin D. Wannamaker, Anthroposophic Press, Spring Valley, New York 1978
The Philosophy of Freedom (The Philosophy of Spiritual Activity). The basis for a modern world conception. Some results of introspective observation following the methods of natural science [*Die Philosophie der Freiheit*, Berlin 1894 and Berlin 1918], translated by Michael Wilson, Rudolf Steiner Press, Forest Row 2006
Theosophy. An Introduction to the Supersensible Knowledge of the World and the Destination of Man [*Theosophie. Einführung in übersinnliche Welterkenntniss und Menschenbestimmung*, Berlin 1904], translated by M. Cotterell, Rudolf Steiner Press, London 1989
How to Know Higher Worlds [*Wie Erlangt Man Erkenntnisse der Höheren Welten?* Berlin 1909 and Berlin 1918], translated by Christopher Bamford, Anthroposophic Press, Great Barrington 1994

An Outline of Esoteric Science [*Die Geheimwissenschaft im Umriß*, Leipzig 1910 and Dornach 1925], translated by Catherine E. Creeger, Anthroposophic Press, Great Barrington 1997

Riddles of the Soul [*Von Seelenrätseln*, Berlin 1917], translated by William Lindeman, Mercury Press, Spring Valley 1999. Extracts from this book also translated into English by Owen Barfield under the title *The Case for Anthroposophy*, Rudolf Steiner Press, London 1970. See also *Von Seelenrätseln. Einführungen von Herbert Witzenmann*, Gideon Spicker Verlag, Dornach 2000. Not currently available in English translation

Witzenmann, Herbert

Pupilship in the Sign of the Rose-Cross. The Individual in Balance as a Builder of Community, translated by Sophia Walsh, Gideon Spicker Verlag, Dornach 1983

Idea and Reality of a Spiritual Schooling of Man. The methodically modern groundwork towards a spiritually scientific university, translated by Virginia Brett, edited by Sophia Walsh, Spicker Books, Northridge, CA, 1986

Intuition and Observation. The aesthetic process examined as a pattern for the grasping of ideals, the discovery of self and the building of community, translated by Sophia Walsh, Spicker Books, Northridge, CA, 1986

Strukturphänomenologie. Vorbewußtes Gestaltbilden im erkennenden Wirklichkeitenthüllen [*Structural Phenomenology. Form-building in the cognitive uncovering of reality*], Gideon Spicker Verlag, Dornach 1983. Not currently available in English translation.

Was ist Meditation? Eine grundlegende Eröterung zur geistes-wissenschaftlichen Bewußtseinserweiterung [*What is Meditation? A fundamental discussion towards the spirit-scientific expansion of consciousness*], Gideon Spicker Verlag, Dornach 1989. Not currently available in English translation.

Der Urgedanke. Rudolf Steiners Zivilisationsprinzip und die Aufgabe der Anthroposophischen Gesellschaft [*The Archetypal Thought. Rudolf*

Steiner's Principle of Civilization and the task of the Anthroposophical Society], Gideon Spicker Verlag, Dornach 1988. Not currently available in English translation.

Reference

The New Oxford Dictionary of English, edited by Judy Pearsall, Clarenden Press, Oxford 1998

NOTES

Part I

1. Rudolf Steiner essentially devoted the chapter 'Are there Limits to Knowledge?' from his *The Philosophy of Spiritual Activity* to making this point. For example, he writes there: 'The preconditions for the coming into being of cognition are therefore *through* and *for* the I. The latter sets itself the questions of cognition. And indeed it takes them from the entirely clear and transparent element of thinking. If we ask questions we cannot answer, the content of the questions cannot be clear and distinct in all their details. It is not the world which poses us questions, but rather we ourselves.' Chapter VII, para. 8. All translations from *The Philosophy of Spiritual Activity* are by the author.

2. Edmund Husserl concerned himself extensively with issues related to thinking and its relationship with the world. He sought to intimate a solution to the problem of *cognition* by demonstrating that 'experience' could become certain 'evidence' (or absolute knowledge) only if the emergence of this experience into consciousness was made utterly transparent. Furthermore, he held the conviction that a full knowledge of thinking was not dependent upon knowing its physiological basis, but that thinking experience constituted a valid reality in its own right. He illustrated his belief on numerous occasions, usually based on the observation that there is no substitute for experiencing something directly. He wrote, for example, that 'A "seeing" [*Schauen*] cannot be demonstrated. The blind man who wishes to see cannot be made to see by means of scientific proofs. Physical and physiological theories about colours give no "seeing" clarity about the meaning of colour as those with

eyesight have it. If, therefore, the critique of cognition is a science, as it doubtless is in the light of these considerations, a science which is to clarify all species and forms of cognition, *it can make no use of any science of a natural sort*. It cannot tie itself to the conclusions that any natural science has reached about what is. For it they remain in question.' Husserl, Edmund, *The Idea of Phenomenology*, transl. William Alston and George Nakhnikian, The Hague 1964, p. 4.

3. This mode of questioning is not without significance. If we adhere to it, we cannot truly say that the world presents us with mysteries we cannot solve. Though this may seem a mystery in itself, we must nonetheless say that if we ask a question of the world we cannot answer it means that we have stepped beyond the bounds of our immediate experience. The content of our question must itself have a dimension that we ourselves have invented as unknowable. This may seem striking, indefensible even, but if we ask a question we cannot answer it is because of the limitations and assumptions implicit in the question, and not through any intrinsic weakness in either our senses or our thinking.

4. Steiner illustrates this point in the chapter 'Thinking in the Service of Understanding the World' from *The Philosophy of Spiritual Activity* through the following example: 'There are people who say: Whether or not our thinking is right in itself, we cannot establish with certainty. In so far as this is concerned, as a point of departure it must therefore remain doubtful. But that is just as reasonably put as if one raised doubts as to whether in itself a tree is right or wrong. Thinking is a fact; and to speak of the rightness or wrongness of a fact is senseless. At most, I can have doubts as to whether thinking is being applied correctly, as I can doubt whether a certain tree and its corresponding wood is suitable for making a particular tool. To show to what extent the application of thinking to the world is right or wrong is just the task of this book. I can understand when someone raises doubts that thinking is able

to settle anything about the world; but to me it is incomprehensible how anyone can doubt the rightness of thinking itself.' Chapter III, para. 32.

5. Steiner explores this notion in the chapter 'Thinking as a Higher Experience within Experience', from his *A Theory of Knowledge*. For example, we read there: 'With respect to the rest of experience, that which enters as an appearance before my consciousness does not at once manifest the whole reality; but, with respect to thought, the whole thing passes over without residue into what is given to me. In the first case, I must penetrate the shell in order to reach the kernel; in the second, shell and kernel are an indivisible unity. It is only a universally human preconception if thought at first appears to us to be entirely analogous with the rest of experience. In the case of thought, we need only overcome this preconception within ourselves. In the case of the rest of experience, we need to resolve a difficulty inherent in the fact itself. /That for which we seek, in the case of the rest of experience, has itself in the case of thinking become immediate experience. /A difficulty is thereby resolved which could scarcely be resolved in any other way.' Chapter VIII, paras. 4, 5 and 6. Transl. Olin. D. Wannamaker.

6. Steiner makes this point in both *A Theory of Knowledge* and *The Philosophy of Spiritual Activity*. For example, in the former we find: 'Amid the unrelated chaos of experience—and, indeed, at first as a fact of experience—we find an element that leads us out beyond this unrelatedness. This element is thought. Thought, as one of the facts of experience, assumes an exceptional position within experience.' Ibid., Chapter VIII, para 1. And from the latter: 'That is the singular nature of thinking, that the thinker forgets thinking while doing it. It is not thinking which occupies him, but rather the object of thinking which he observes. /The first observation we can make regarding thinking is that it is the unobserved element in our ordinary thinking life [*Geistesleben*]. /The reason why we

do not observe thinking in daily thinking life is none other than because it depends upon our own activity.' Chapter III, paras. 11, 12 and 13.

7. The unravelling of the *Gorgon Knot* of *thinking about thinking* is one of the great philosophical achievements of Rudolf Steiner's book *The Philosophy of Spiritual Activity*. In the third chapter, 'Thinking in the Service of Understanding the World', Steiner writes the following: 'The reason which makes it impossible for us to observe thinking at any moment during its current course is the same as that which allows us to know it more directly and more intimately than any other process in the world. Just because we ourselves bring it forth means that we know the character of its course, the way in which the resulting process takes place. What in other spheres of observation can only be found indirectly: the factually corresponding context [*sachlich-entsprechende Zusammenhang*] and the relationship between individual objects—in the case of thinking we know in an absolutely direct way.' Chapter III, para. 16. And also: 'When Archimedes had discovered the lever, he believed that with its help he could lift the whole cosmos from its hinges, if only he could find a point from which to support his instrument. He needed something which could be supported through itself, and not through something else. In thinking we have a principle which exists through itself. From here on the search will be to understand the world. We are able to grasp thinking through itself. The question is only whether, through the same [principle], we are able to comprehend anything else.' Chapter III, para. 29.

Part II

1. Such assumptions as these were very much the concern of the young Rudolf Steiner working at the end of the nineteenth century. However, they are still very much with us at the beginning of the twenty-first century. For example, in the first

paragraph of Chapter VI of his *Philosophy of Spiritual Activity*, Steiner wrote: 'The question: how do I gain information from the tree which stands ten paces away from where I stand is completely inappropriately put. It stems from the point of view that the boundaries of my body are barrier walls through which objects' messages wander into me.'

2. A concept is similar to an idea. In the present context we use the word concept to describe something more general and more abstract than we usually understand by the word idea. However, the distinction is a subtle one, and so much so that the two words can virtually be used interchangeably.

3. This is an adaptation of a phrase used by Herbert Witzenmann in many of his philosophical works: *eine Totalexistenz im Universum*. For example, in his book *Was ist Meditation?* we read: 'Through our thinking participation in the shaping of the world as it appears, we have thereby to do with a total existence in the universe—in fact its immeasurable content and extent is never fully in consciousness (since we can always only realize a part of the total), but is more or less subconscious, though its sense of being is founded on clear cognition. "Tat twam asi", "You are that": this Brahminical saying brings this view of the world to expression. And in our observing of our cognitive shaping of the world we bring to consciousness this sense of being connected with the world as it appears.' From *Was ist Meditation?*, Section 5. Translation is by the author.

Part III

1. Such a state is probably impossible, since we cannot survive without the movement of our breath. Nevertheless, the point is clear that were we to be entirely passive, our state of being awake to the world would still entail a flow of thoughts, one into another. That is, even when we are perfectly still, we are awake to the world through a sense of *inner* movement.

2. Of course there are profound mysteries behind our experience

of time. Edmund Husserl (1859–1938), the founder of modern phenomenology, made an exhaustive study of the consciousness of time, and how it comes into being. He took as his primary starting point the experience of a melody, beginning with a minute study of how we can experience a continuous tone as a unified entity, even though we only ever hear what Husserl terms a now-phase of that tone. Among the many interesting observations he makes is the following: 'Every new now is precisely new and is characterized as new phenomenologically. Even if the tone continues so utterly unchanged that not the least alteration is apparent to us, hence even if each new now possesses precisely the same apprehension-content with respect to moments of quality, intensity, etc., and carries precisely the same apprehension—even if all of this is the case, an original difference nevertheless presents itself, a difference that belongs to a new dimension. And this difference is a continuous one . . . This continuum of modifications in the apprehension-content and the apprehensions built on them produces the consciousness of the extension of the tone together with the continual sinking into the past of what is already extended.' Husserl, Edmund, *On the Phenomenology of the Consciousness of Internal Time (1893–1917)*, transl. John Barnett Brough, Dordrecht 1991, p. 67.

3. Husserl also makes this same point: 'The perception of something real is itself something real, and their times coincide. The now of the perception is identically the same as the now of the perceived; the duration of the perception is identical with the duration of the perceived, and so forth. If the perceived is *something transcendent, then*, even if it is not really [*reell*] given, it *appears* in precisely the same now in which the perception, which does become really given itself, exists.' Ibid., p. 284.

4. The philosopher Franz Brentano (1838–1917), who was something of a mentor for the young Rudolf Steiner at the University of Vienna, also investigated the problem of time. In

his unpublished manuscripts on time he, too, took as his starting point the observation that major discrepancies exist between what the senses receive in terms of impressions and the nature of our actual experience. He expressed this distinction very succinctly when he observed that *the duration of a sensation and the sensation of duration are quite different*. See Husserl, ibid., p. 12.

5. Generally speaking, the more we bring these processes to consciousness, thereby revealing more of our thinking activity to us, the slower our sense of unfolding time. Conversely, in the absence of awareness, such as during deep sleep or in a somnambulistic state, our sense of passing time is almost entirely lost, whereby an hour can seem like a minute. The opposite can also *appear* to be the case, when, for example, we dose off for an instant but experience a whole sequence of events apparently lasting longer than the actual time passed. But such moments are also ones of reduced self-awareness.

6. We may, of course, be mistaken if, say, we are on a stage or film set where the room is not strictly speaking a room at all, or we are faced with a plastic replica of a tree which we mistakenly believe to be a real tree. Some of the problems associated with true and false recognition will be looked at in Part IV.

7. This line of reasoning is based partly on a passage from Steiner's book *Theosophy*, first published in Berlin in 1904, in which he describes the following picture: 'My eye perceives the colour of the rose only as long as the rose is in front of it and my eye is itself open. The presence of the things of the outer world as well as of the bodily organs are necessary in order that an impression, a sensation or a perception can occur. But what I have recognized in my intellect as truth concerning the rose does not pass with the present moment.' See Rudolf Steiner, *Theosophy*, transl. M. Cotterell, Chapter II, para. 1.

8. Husserl, describing the experience of the successive tones of a melody, writes the following: 'Must we not say: When the

second tone sounds, I hear *it*, but I no longer hear the first, etc.? In truth, then, I do not hear the melody but only the single present tone. That the elapsed part of the melody is something objective for me, I owe—or so one will be inclined to say—to memory; and that I do not presuppose, with the appearance of the currently intended tone, that this is *all*, I owe to anticipatory expectation.' Husserl, ibid., pp. 24–5.

9. Husserl makes the same observation in the following terms: 'As shocking (when not initially even absurd) as it may seem to say that the flow of consciousness constitutes its own unity, it is nonetheless the case that it does and that this is something that can be made intelligible on the basis of the flow's essential constitution.' Ibid., p. 390.

10. If we are blind, we may form our mental picture of the chairs by touching them. The resulting mental pictures may therefore have an emphasis towards the tactile rather than the visual; but this in no way diminishes any sense of reality regarding the chairs. The universal concept 'chair' will have been individualized with a different emphasis to the clear-sighted person; but the blind person is no less able to reflect upon the conceptual processes from which their pictures are formed, thus giving them equal access to the total world existence in a universalized form. The sensorily impaired person is therefore no more removed from reality than anyone else, since the coming together of inherent concept with universal concept which is the source of our sense of reality is, by definition, beyond any faculty of visualization. It is a faculty of thinking, not of sense perception. All that the sensorily impaired person may lack are certain dimensions of vivacity to their pictures of the world. But every one of us is prone to that to some degree.

11. This unification of the perception and thinking is one of the principal themes of Steiner's *The Philosophy of Spiritual Activity*. For example, in the chapter 'Are There Limits to Knowledge?' we read: 'First when the egohood [*die Ichheit*] has combined for itself the two elements of reality which, in the world, are

inseparably combined, does cognitive satisfaction then occur: the I [*das Ich*] has again arrived at reality.' Chapter VII, para. 7.

12. Although this chapter undoubtedly has parallels with passages from Rudolf Steiner's book *Theosophy*, such as those describing our experience of the flowers of a meadow, I have tried my best to put such passages out of my mind and write something out of myself. The similarities, however, are not coincidental; but nor, I hope, are they a sign that I have in any way copied Steiner's style or approach in this case.

Part IV

1. The notion of a mental picture or mental representation is one which has dominated Western philosophy through the centuries. Rudolf Steiner, in Chapter VI of his *Philosophy of Spiritual Activity*, defined a mental picture (*Vorstellung*) as 'an individualized concept'. The problem of stepping beyond our mental pictures is also investigated by Steiner in the book *Von Seelenrätseln* [*From the Riddles of the Soul*] (1917). However, the notion of a mental picture is such that, whatever the definition, since it is a mental faculty which everybody can experience, direct engagement with the concept should always be seen as vastly preferable to any fixed form of words to describe it.

2. These examples should also serve to warn us against believing that it is primarily our senses and their apparent limitations which are at fault. Each of the examples described is not a failing of our senses but of the way we think about what our senses offer us. For such moments of miscognizing, of recognizing based upon surface appearance alone, of mistaking one thing for another, of projecting an object into space when really there is nothing there, or of being unable to recognize at all what the world presents us with, are failings in thinking, not of sense perception.

3. The relationship between feeling (and the soul in general) and

the human bodily organism was given a whole new dimension of clarity by Rudolf Steiner in his book *Von Seelenrätseln*. In what is ostensibly a footnote to the main body of the text discreetly titled 'The physical and spiritual dependencies of the human being', Steiner writes for the first time of his threefold conception of the human being. As regards our feeling life, Steiner introduces the notion that changes in what we might call our rhythmic system are the source of a feeling, and not the other way round (that a feeling, as some form of psychic event, instigates a change in our body) as one might expect. Thus, 'when something is "pictured", a nerve process takes place, on the basis of which the soul becomes conscious of what is pictured; further to this, when something is "felt", a modification in the rhythm of breathing takes place, through which the soul revives (*auflebt*) a feeling; and *so* it goes on, that when something is "willed", a metabolic process precedes it, which is the corporeal foundation for that which is experienced in the soul as willing.' See Steiner, R., *Von Seelenrätseln*, Gideon Spicker Verlag, Dornach 2000, pp. 108–9. Translations from this book are by the author.

4. Rudolf Steiner proposes a similar notion of non-picturing in *Von Seelenrätseln*. In a descriptive example of the problem of experiencing willing, which is also applicable to feeling, Steiner writes: 'Mental picture building is experienced somewhat as if one sees an area painted with colour; willing is like a black area within a coloured field. One "sees" something inside the area where there is no colour, just because, in contrast to the surroundings from which sensations of colour arise, from the black area no such impressions come: one "brings forth an image of willing", because at certain moments soul experiences of mental pictures are enriched by a non-picturing which inserts itself into fully conscious experience in a similar way to how the conscious course of life is broken by sleep's interruptions of consciousness.' Ibid., p. 109.

5. The faculty being described here is essentially the same as that

which Rudolf Steiner often referred to as inspiration. In the present work I have purposely avoided the words imagination, inspiration and intuition (as used by Rudolf Steiner in many contexts), instead wishing to develop my own words and phrases out of my own approach to these different faculties. Thus, my own *using thinking as a sense organ in its own right* is close to imagination, while *bringing together the life processes as we experience them in the world with the inner movement of our own being* (along with other phrases) is close to inspiration. The latter also concurs with the way in which inspiration is sometimes called figuratively 'the reading of the occult script.' For Rudolf Steiner's own descriptions of these terms see, for example, the chapter 'The Perception of Higher Worlds' from *Occult Science in Outline*.

6. Rudolf Steiner also puts forward this radical notion in Chapter IX of his book *The Philosophy of Spiritual Activity*. There he writes: 'To the essential being, which works in thinking, there applies a double nature: the first is to push back the human organism in its own activity; and secondly, to set itself in its place. For also the first, the pushing back of the bodily organization, is the result of thought activity.'

7. Rudolf Steiner speaks of a soul body in his book *Theosophy*. See for example the sub-chapter 'Body, Soul and Spirit'. There Steiner defines the soul body in relation to the human etheric body, which is not a concept I touch upon in this context. The derivation of the notion of a soul body in the present work is therefore quite different from that presented by Steiner. However, I believe that the two derivations, though essentially different, still yield complementary results.

8. The question of mind and body, or mind and brain, is one in relation to which diametrically opposed and trenchant views exist. The present study, from its thinking perspective, suggests only that the activity of the brain which we are able to investigate physically in all its complexity is a receding of the physical world such that thinking activity can arise in the

negative space which arises in its place. In other words, investigations of brain activity should proceed on this basis, rather than believing that the visible physical activity is the thoughts themselves. Furthermore, the fact that if the brain is damaged and certain specific (and predictable) mental faculties are altered is not entirely different from when our other sense organs are damaged and the perceptions which pass through them are altered. On its own, the correlation between physical brain activity and mental activity is not enough to establish that the physical brain is constitutive of human thinking. At most it can only establish that it is regulative of it. A similar point is made by Rudolf Steiner in Chapter IX of his *Philosophy of Spiritual Activity*. See note 6 above.

9. One might say that fantasy is the melding of all of these. However, the faculty of fantasizing, though it enables us to be creative, does so at the expense of allowing us to lose sight of reality. It is like the gift of fire to the human race in that it can be used both creatively and destructively.

Part V

1. Notions of freedom held by one group of people may be quite different from, or inappropriate to, those held by another. For example, for one group freedom of choice in all its various manifestations may appear to be the only practical notion of freedom available. As far as their definition or understanding of freedom is concerned, they may, to themselves at least, appear to have many freedoms in terms of where they shop and what they buy, also in what they read or in what they wear. Likewise, in their eyes, those for whom these same freedoms are not available or have been denied are therefore less free. However, such freedoms of choice are not necessarily transferable to all contexts. A group of people living off the land in a remote location may have no need for shops or money. Indeed, the very notion of a shop may be alien to them, as may

be reading or having a large choice of clothes to wear. What is more, when we follow a similar course of reasoning but in the opposite direction by asking ourselves the question 'If we increase the choice available to someone, do we make them more free?' the matter becomes no clearer. Again, the notion is relative to the context in which it is being asked. Indeed, the final absurdity seems to come when we ask the question 'If we were to furnish someone with unlimited choice, would we thereby make them free?'